Golden Years
of
KEIGHLEY

TRUE NORTH BOOKS
DEAN CLOUGH
HALIFAX
WEST YORKS
HX3 5AX
TEL. 01422 344344
WWW.NOSTALGIA-BOOKS.CO.UK

First published in Great Britain by:
True North Books, Dean Clough, Halifax HX3 5AX
1998

ISBN 1 900 463 92 x

© Copyright: True North Books

This book is published in association with:

Harrison & Clough Limited

Golden Years of Keighley

Text	*Kevin McIlroy*
Text pages design	*Mandy Walker*
Photographs compiled by	*Phil Holland*
Cover design	*Mark Smith*
Business development	*Stuart Glenholmes*

Contents

Acknowledgments

The publishers would like to thank

Mrs Pauline Barfield

Mr Ian Dewhirst

Keighley Local Studies Library

Mr D Prior

*An aerial view from the Parish Church of the south end of
the town towards West Lane in 1966.*

Introduction

Producing another book of nostalgic reflections on the Keighley we used to know was a challenge taken up enthusiastically by everyone involved. Where possible we have tried to concentrate upon a period within the memory of most of our readers; the 1940s, 50s and 60s - decades which saw tremendous changes in the town, and a time when changes in the world of work, entertainment, public health and retailing. *Change* takes place constantly in every town and Keighley is no exception.

As we all get older it is often easier to 'step back' and view events and developments with a clearer sense of perspective. Our aim has been to assist in this respect by presenting a 'catalyst' capable of rekindling memories of days gone by in an entertaining manner. Looking through the pages of this book it may be surprising how much change has taken place, and over such a relatively short period, relative to the long history of the area. Street scenes are not neglected. Photographs of this nature were popular in the last book, and understandably so. The changing face of the town is reflected in the way our roads and shops have developed to meet the changing needs of our lives over the years. These photographs show the shops and motorcars we remember from our early days, along with the fashions which were all the rage when we were younger. All combine to refresh our memories of days gone by, and when that occurs the book will have achieved its aim.

Events & occasions

Below: Once the young man at the door can make up his mind whether he wants to be in the photograph then there will a decent shot of this gathering. The boy scout sneaking in the front row is not helping either. Charlie Miller and his Airedale Players are ready and the Saturday dance in January 1938 can get underway. The theme this year is 'Airplanes' and the National School hall at the bottom of West Lane is 'tastefully decorated' in pink, blue and silver. For many years previous to this the Keighley Parish Church Sunday School had organised these Conversaziones, or 'Cons', as they were popularly known, at the beginning of each year. They were originally started in 1875 in order to help to pay off the debt on the Keighley Mechanics Institute and over the years their popularity increased. It became a week of entertainment, of exhibitions, parties for the children, fancy dress balls and this dance on the final Saturday evening. At a time when entertainment was not pre-packaged these kinds of events would be a much looked forward-to social highlight.

So in a year in which the Walt Disney cartoon film, 'Snow White and the Seven Dwarfs' was judged unsuitable for children's viewing as some of the scenes in it were termed to be too visually horrific for them and BBC screened two versions of Wagner's opera, 'Tristan' and Blackpool's North Pier Pavilion was destroyed by fire and Great Britain and Germany eyed each other up before war, the adults and the not so old in the hall can once again have a good night out.

Right: The Mayor and Mayoress of Keighley, Councillor and Mrs W E Walton look thoroughly at home at the 1958 edition of the Saturday afternoon carnival and gala of the Keighley Mechanics Institute Conversaziones, 'Cons' for short, held appropriately in the Municipal Hall. Time and change of social habits are two of the reasons why these events are just a memory now. Six hundred and fifty children and two hundred and fifty adults attended this year's event and as they, or most of them, pose happily for the photographer, you have to wonder 'Where are all the boys?' But at that age then and in those days many a little girl might have said aloud 'Who needs boys?' while secretly thinking the opposite possibly. The show must go on, however. There is the fancy-dress competition, the puppet show and what is always the highlight of the Saturday gala the grand march round the hall. The organisation for this event, both beforehand and especially during must have been thorough and tiring. Fancy trying to get that number of children to all do the same thing at the same time. But judging by their smiles the bow-tied organisers do not seem to mind and there is always the Saturday evening dance for them to look forward to.

Above: If you want to be a nurse when you grow up why not practise with the real ones? Especially if it's the Princess Royal visiting Keighley and she is coming to met the Red Cross and she is the Commander in Chief of the British Detachments.

The Spitfire-Hurricane fund, so successful three years earlier, was superseded by the 'Wings For Victory Week' appeal which now had a positive ring to it as the allies went on the offensive against the Germans. The appeal indicator set up in the Town Hall Square showed the town's target to be £750,000, the 'cost of ten Lancaster bombers and seventy-five Spitfire fighters.' By the Wednesday, the day of the royal visit, it registered £897,529. The presence of a member of the Royal Family in those days was a special event as it would be some time before royal lives were regularly put on public display. Queen Elizabeth had visited Steeton in 1942 and now it was the turn of the Princess. She carried out other engagements while she was here. There was an inspection of the guard of honour of the Keighley Girls' Training Corps of the Women's Auxiliary Air Force. There was a visit to the Hospital Supplies Depot, the headquarters of the Women's Voluntary Service and to the Woodbine Day Nursery.

The special week had begun with a parade of Voluntary organisations and auxiliary services and it finished on Saturday May 22nd 1943 with Keighley's response showing a magnificent £1,453,147. It is because of efforts like these that Britain's fighting forces were able to make such an offensive and to ensure ultimate victory.

Right: The story of the flying ship, Hindenburgh, and its unscheduled flight over the north of England was as mysterious as it was intriguing.

Its regular flight path from New Jersey in the United States to its German home in Frankfurt took a 'wrong' turn on its journey east on May 16th 1936 and it passed over Barrow in Furness, Bradford, Leeds and finally Keighley, where she dropped a package containing carnations, a silver and jet crucifix, a picture of a flying boat, postage stamps and a sheet of Hindenburg notepaper.

There was a message from John P Shulte, who said he was a priest, to the finder to place the crucifix and carnations on the grave of his brother, Lieutenant Franz Shulte, a first world war prisoner who died in 1919 and was buried in Morton Cemetery.

Naturally in the tension between Britain and Germany at that time the whole affair was regarded with a certain amount of suspicion, especially as the plane had flown over a shipyard and the industrial towns and cities of the north. This photograph is of her second journey across the region westward on June 16th taken, like many others of it, from Utley.

The Hindenburgh was the biggest airship in the world at eight hundred and four feet long filled with hydrogen with a capacity of seven million cubic feet. It even boasted a dance floor. The Zeppelin, as she termed at the time, was destroyed by fire in 1938 when an explosion occurred as she was mooring at Lakehurst in New Jersey, resulting in the death of fifty of the hundred occupants who were on board.

Annual works outings were popular in the days when cars were a luxury that many could not afford and holidays were a rare event even to the British seaside never mind abroad. Cook's World Wide Travel Service were soon to offer two weeks in Italy for £48.10.6 or eight days in Paris for £22.19. If you were rich or had just won the treble chance on Littlewoods or Vernons Pools you could fly to Australia for £240 but having endured the food and power shortages that made 1947 such a bleak year you might wish soon to emigrate to that country at a cost of £10. But it is the year that Princess Elizabeth and Philip had just announced their engagement in July and the wedding of that popular couple will be in November. Things can only get better. Don Bradman and the other Australian cricketers are here next year and there is always the game against Norman Yardley's Yorkshire team and the test match. All you have to do is to queue for hours to get in but it will be worth it. Bradman always scores a few at Headingley. So, despite the chilly weather and armed with raincoats to the fore and plenty of smiles all round, the staff of Robert Clough Ltd can have their day out like the 400 staff of the Keighley Co-op who went to Blackpool in fourteen coaches and the Master Bakers Association who opted for Scarborough and the Boot Trades Association who visited Robin Hood country, the Dukeries.

Above: Eleven boys and seven girls who made up the athletics team to represent Holycroft School at the Keighley Elementary School Sports in 1934 sit proudly on the school steps with their cups and shields. Equally as proud at the back is the Headteacher, Mr William E Walton, and raising a smile are teachers, Mr Barker and Miss Bracewell. They had every reason to be pleased. The team had come first. The girls' relay team had won the RV Marriner trophy and the mixed relay team ran well to win the Mrs Craven Laycock trophy. The comment about the team's performance and win was that it was 'somewhat phenomenal'. Whatever description is given, it certainly deserved a reward from the head - being let home early, an extra day's holiday even. Who knows? This was the time of minimum official interference in how schools were run and perhaps if Mr Walton thought it was all right, then that would be fine. It would be difficult to compare the education these boys and girls received with that on offer for children two generations later when Mr Walton would have more than the local 'office' influencing the way he was running the school and when paper work often appears more important to some members of officialdom than teaching children. To these children of Holycroft School league tables meant that they were first and Highfield School was eighteen points behind. That is why it was 'phenomenal'.

Below: 'Keighley is apparently making a reputation for producing expert players on the piano-accordion' so observed the Keighley News in 1936. The town's musical tradition of singing and playing was being further enhanced by the men who took up playing this and other 'new' instruments. It was estimated at this time there were about fifty accordionists in the Keighley Accordion Club which met in the Temperance Hall. The groups or bands they formed became an outstanding feature of the musical and social life of the area. There was the Jack Wilson's eleven strong Harmonica and Accordion Band, regulars at Keighley Galas, whose 'trademark' was the growing in popularity Latin-American music and their costume reflected their musical style. There was the Keighley Concertina Band which at one time had more than thirty members and could be regularly heard from the bandstands of Victoria Park and Lund Park. The band here is the Rialto Harmonica and Accordion Band with Charlie Oaks on piano and, from left to right, Jack Nicholson, Charlie Johnson, Maurice Nicholson, Billy Talent and Billy Hensman. One of the Nicholsons with Charlie Johnson and Billy Hensman, together with Bernard Really, formed the 'Four Hensman Boys' and won 3rd prize in the then famous Carrol Levis radio talent show in Bradford. As a result they were promised a visit to London to broadcast but they only got as far as the BBC studios in Woodhouse Lane in Leeds.

Above: Busy days for Keighley firemen in August 1969 began on the Tuesday with a blaze at the Haworth Scouring Company's Lees Mills in the village and four days later it dealt with a similar outbreak at the Hayfield Mills of John Horsfall in Glusburn. But the biggest fire Keighley had ever known was sandwiched between the two when what can only be described as a raging inferno destroyed the Beech Mills of worsted spinners, Thomas Hird and Sons, of Halifax Road. It took 25 pumps and 125 firemen from all the local stations and also from as far afield as Harrogate to tackle the fire. There were no workers injured fortunately although six firemen needed treatment. The fire caused £1 million of damage and the effect of the fire on the surrounding area was as one person stated 'unbelievable'. Trees in the Knowle Chapel of Rest were set on fire as were those in the driveway of Taylor's Brewery. Sparks landed on the roofs of houses as far away as Queens Road. Halifax Road was closed for the next three days. The effect on the workers who had just returned from their annual holiday could have been worse for most were absorbed into the firm's Knowle Mill nearby. They had to read the news on a notice pinned to a telegraph pole outside their burnt-out mill. Fires at three mills in four days was put down to coincidence but to crown it all there was another mill fire at Bethel Rhodes's Alice Street Mills on the following Monday. Quite a few days!

Above right: Onlookers stand sadly in the snow in February 1956 at the scene of Keighley's worst-ever blaze. Eight people, including six women, died as the fire at the four storey Eastwood Mills of the worsted spinners, Robert C. Franklin Ltd swept through the building. At

its height 15 appliances from 10 brigades tackled the fire, and flames, fanned by a stiff breeze, reached heights of over one hundred feet. These spectators were forced to retreat at one stage due to the intense heat and falling masonry. The bravery of Henry Fielden, who lived near-by, saved the lives of three female employees when they were trapped on an upper floor. He smashed down a door and, despite the heat and the smoke from the fire which was made even worse as the floors were impregnated with oil, managed to lead them to safety. He was quite a reluctant hero for after his heroics he just went home and it was only later the story of his bravery was told. Panic had set in as workers fled to safety and police cars had to tour the streets telling employees to return to the mill so that a roll-call could be taken. The repercussions of the fire lasted for some time. The local MP, Charles Hobson, asked questions in Parliament about fire safety procedures and inspections at that mill in particular and old mills in general and the fire brigade had to re-think its practices in dealing with fires in buildings like this one. All in all it was a sad day for Keighley.

Keighley firemen tackle a lunchtime blaze at the Low Bridge Worsted Spinning Mills of Thomas Wilson (Keighley) Ltd. in April 1965. The fire was not as spectacular, if any fire is spectacular, as other mill blazes but it was one of a series of mill fires at this time. It was confined to one small room containing packaging material and, fortunately, there was no damage to the wool. That did not stop onlookers in Sun Street having to move away because of the thick smoke which forced firemen to wear breathing apparatus. The local brigade had moved into its new premises on Bradford Road during the previous year after occupying its Coney Lane site since the end of the last century when it took over building once owned by the gas company. Planning naturally preceded action and the first plan to move was considered in 1916 but the brigade did not move from even then inadequate and unsuitable premises. There was much talk before the war of a new station but no action. It was highlighted again in 1949 but the plan was dropped. But in 1962 work began on a modern six bay appliance building. It had good access and was close to the then direct roads to Silsden and Bingley. Two years later after 76 years of waiting, Keighley had a new station. The opening ceremony was interrupted by a call-out to Hebden and Holdings on North Street when rubbish had caught fire. So much for planning!

Left: The gas offices are in full array to celebrate the Coronation of King George 6th in May 1937 as the town and the country overcome the then trauma of the three hundred and twenty-five day reign of his brother, Edward 8th. In the previous year George 5th had died. His successor, Edward, abdicated and his younger son became king. It is hard to imagine today that the effect of Edward's decision not to give up his relationship with Mrs Simpson, an American divorcee, would cause so much turmoil in this country and abroad. Times have changed and similar events today might not have brought similar repercussions. But there was national distress and Edward's 'final and irrevocable' decision to give up the crown for the sake of a woman he loved has all the makings of a Hollywood movie except it was true and it was important to the country and to the Empire. The father of our present Queen, a shy retiring man, was suddenly thrust into the national limelight and he and his wife Elizabeth, now Queen Mother, became King and Queen. The affection and acclaim shown to them and to their two daughters, Elizabeth and Margaret Rose was as much due to loyalty as to a collective sigh of relief that the year when we had three kings was soon to be forgotten. The celebrations nationally and locally were long and heartfelt. Streets and buildings were decorated hence the gas office's

display. The only thing which might have marred it was the prize for Keighley's best decorated premises went to the Electricity offices.

Below: 'Have you ever had an embarrassing moment?' 'Are you courting?' 'What's on the table, Mabel?' 'If you had three wishes, what would they be?' These questions could only have come from the lips of Halifax's own Wilfred Pickles, star compere of radio's popular show, 'Have A Go' to the staff of Grove Mills in their canteen. But all is not what it seems.
This is not the radio show. It is Wilfred and the Crown Film Unit filming 'The Golden Fleece' for the then Ministry of Labour, produced to encourage people to enter the growing textile industry. Robert Clough Ltd had been chosen as a good location and a hundred lucky employees were given a friday off work on that August day in 1948 to take part as extras. All the famous 'Have A Go' features were included and being asked those questions, and more, are contestants, spinners Anne Davidson, Lorna Metcalfe and Marjorie Leach, together with the firm's long-serving chief clerk, Arthur Smith. Standing next to Wilfred, looking as though this is his most embarrassing moment is overlooker, Donald Lee. It was he, however, who stoutly declared in the film that his firm made the finest quality cloth in Yorkshire. 'Give him the money, Barney.'

Below: The only way to show off these six wheelchairs which had been presented in 1948 to the Keighley St John's Ambulance Brigade by members of the local Inner Wheel was for the photographer, William Speight, to use healthy volunteers to act as models. The work of voluntary organisations like the ambulance brigade was of vital importance immediately after the war. In 1947 this country endured one of the worst winters on record. There had been a fuel crisis as transport had been dislocated and coal production was badly reduced. People queued for coke at the Keighley Corporation Gas Depot. Electricity cuts had led to a run on candles and the gas mains pressure was reduced. That year Britons led a bleak existence. It is hard to imagine today that there could have been a shortage of food and goods in the shops and the essentials of life such as heat and power were in short supply. An age of austerity indeed. It is against this background that the Labour programme to change Britain was put into action with the introduction of the national insurance scheme to support family allowance and retirement or widow's pension and the establishment of an all embracing health service as the state accepted a larger responsibility for the individual citizen. But the state could not, and still cannot, do everything and the reliance on voluntary efforts to fund essential services like health and social welfare has always been part of the national way of life. Hence the necessity for such organisations as the St

John's Ambulance and the recognition of groups like the Inner Wheel that support is mutual.

Right: As the Battle of Britain took its toll of our fighting men and of the aircraft they flew, it became a matter of desperation that if we were to repel the German Luftwaffe should need to replace the aircraft to defend our country. A national Spitfire-Hurricane campaign was established in 1940 and once again Keighley's traditional generosity was tested to the full. By means of concerts, garden parties, bring and buy sales, what seemed to be miles of pennies and collections, plus other individual efforts to which children of the day showed a great enthusiasm and loyalty, Keighley set out to raise the necessary funds. One novel means of collecting was a 15 feet by 10 feet drawing of an aeroplane in the Town Hall Square and the public was invited to fill in its outline with coins. This was the age of hardship in terms of the shortage of basic food items but Keighley and its people rallied to the cause and within two months had raised £11,600 which paid for Spitfire and a Hurricane and there was even something left over for the RAF Benevolent Fund. Here in the winter snow we see Keighley's own Hurricane Mark 11a number 22749. Firms and businesses also played their part in the campaign and Dean Smith and Grace raised enough money for a Spitfire which was promptly given the firm's name. As a result of the magnificent efforts of towns like Keighley, Britain gradually assumed the ascendancy of the skies.

Above: Pre-war photographs of Keighley Friendly Societies' Gala processions tended to be extensively photographed. James Dewhirst of the Oakworth Road newsagents and stationers, A Dewhirst and Sons, used to snap participants, then rush out special shop window displays and consequently did a roaring trade in prints. There was enterprise! There is a nautical and topical theme to this 1936 entry as it passes the post office and Charles Hanson's, appropriately a jokes and novelty shop, on a crowded Halifax Road. The fame of the galas bought crowds to the town from other towns and cities in the area, as we can see from the large numbers here at this point, as the procession toured Keighley. The galas attracted entrants of varying degrees of 'madness'. At one time there was the comic band contest with an unofficial competition for the most outlandish band names. Typical of these were the Keighley Wiffum, Waffum, Wuffum Band or the Haworth Bingem Bangem Band or the Otley Splishem Splashem Band or the more mundane Skipton Belle Vue Duffers.

Right: 'The Gala comes but once a year, it gives us such delight, to see the long procession pass, it's such a splendid sight. *(Chorus)* To keep the gala up, to keep the gala up, let each do all that ever he can to keep the gala up.

The gala song of 1936 to drive along the enthusiasm for the Keighley Gala. The originators of the first gala might have had their own song. They had organised the Keighley Friendly Societies Gala for the first time in 1877 to raise money for the Keighley Cottage Hospital and all local groups and organisations were encouraged to enter a float. It became a matter of pride involving weeks of preparation to think of a theme, then prepare the costumes and to make sure you have a vehicle to mount the tableau on and to drive you round Keighley on the procession. Being a hospital charity gala the most enthusiastic participants were the nurses themselves. In 1946 they won second prize with 'Carmen' and in 1948 with 'Carnival in Madrid', another exotic theme they were awarded third prize. This was their 1947 offering.

A bizarre set of characters indeed who did not win any prizes buy they obviously had fun, the real aim of the gala, for that is how to raise the money.

After the end of the war with the coming of the National Health Service and national funding for all medical treatment, the gala changed its name and prime aim when it became the Keighley Charities Gala.

Below: Village life in the age of limited communications and transport was self centred and the village gala was very much a whole community affair with a sense of pulling together. Stanbury Village Galas in the 1930s were typical of these. The participants in this photograph would seem to amuse each other as much as they amused the crowd. Village social life centred very much on the village activities more than today and would include the churches and chapels, the mills, the shops and the public houses. The Local Studies section of Keighley Library contains a fascinating account of Stanbury life, written obviously by someone not only with deep knowledge of the village, but on reading it, a deep attachment to its institutions and traditions. There are detailed accounts of life at Lumbfoot Mill and Hollings Mill, of the growth of the local co-op, of the influence and activities at the Wagon and Horses Inn, the Cross Inn and the Friendly Inn. Scarcroft Sunday School and Chapel's activities are chronicled in detail but the most fascinating title of one pamphlet is 'We Almost Had A Railway', the story of the growth of the local railway system which, as the title suggests, did not reach Stanbury. If every village community had their historical activities logged in this way, and there are a great many who have, they are as interesting to read as any history book. A bit like a village's own family tree.

Right: The 1970 Keighley gala procession is following the traditional route through the town and here we see part of it on Victoria Road. The smartly dressed, black leather shoed cubs under the watchful eye of their cub mistress are taking a keen interest in the crowd and what is going on around them. Catching them up is a selection of veteran and vintage cars from the Peter Black collection. The sight of those cars gives those whose memory can stretch that far back chance to recall the 1952 film 'Genevieve' which had Kenneth More, Kay Kendall, Diana Sheridan and John Gregson as four of its stars, the fifth being the car itself. Tragically Kay Kendall was to die not long afterwards in 1959 aged 32 years. That film, together with people like Peter Black and Lord Montagu, did a great deal to stir up people's enthusiasm for these cars by opening up their collections to the public, although the Veteran Car Club had been in existence since 1930 but was regarded then as rather exclusive. It is always a fine sight to see the cars each year following the route through the Dales on the Keighley to Morecambe Run and the interest they arouse from the spectators who line the route shows that enthusiasm for them and the dress of the drivers and passengers is still strong.

Keighley's proximity to Leeds and Bradford allowed it visits and events that many other small towns could not enjoy. The thrill of the circus was a treat young and old enjoyed. In 1899 the world famous Barnum and Bailey's circus bedazzled Keighley with their 'Greatest Show on Earth', although there was a smallpox epidemic in the north of England at the time. Here on this wet day in 1902 on a recently widened North Street came the parade to announce the arrival of Robert Sanger's Circus.

The people of Keighley could enjoy an actual Big Top, watch clowns, acrobats, tight-rope walkers and that daring young man, or men, on the flying trapeze as well as the elephants, the camels and the dromedaries. The following year after visiting Halifax came William Cody, better known as Buffalo Bill and his Wild West Show, featuring stands for 14000 spectators and 500 horses and all the thrills of a part of the world lauded about then only in books and comics and then rarely visited. That is how often legends are made.

Whether the next visitor was legendary is another matter, for in 1910 came the quaintly named Captain Wombwell, together with a Mr. Bostock and their menagerie which included lions and tigers, a porcupine and a wolf and a bison and a creature supposed to be half lion and half tiger. Unfortunately it died.

Above: Ramsden's Brewery supplied the beer to the Cavendish Hotel in 1967 before its Halifax brewery closed itself a short time later. Things are changing in Keighley too. Judging by the way this lady is crossing Lawkholme Crescent she is not without interest to find out what is going on behind that wooden partition. She and the inquisitive gentleman would see the work has commenced to build a car park. This street contained some of the traditional shop names of the town and now they have disappeared as Keighley tries to come to terms with the demands of the second half of the twentieth century.There is the increase in number of private cars and the inadequacy of the existing streets to cope with it. There is insufficient parking spaces for these cars. Commercial traffic has expanded both in number and size of vehicle. The 'through' traffic to and from towns and cities like Bradford, Halifax and Skipton has to be catered for unless the town comes to a standstill. The public transport system needs space to drive, to stop and to park. So action is needed. Car parks are built. Parking restrictions are multiplied. The needs of the pedestrian have to be considered and the town centre is over a period to undergo a massive change. That Keighley's centre had to change was inevitable. How it was done was important.

Top: At the time when this photograph was taken in 1970 the Cavendish Hotel had been in existence for 70 years. Named after the Cavendish family who as the Dukes of Devonshire were the landowners or lords of the manor for several generations, this purpose built hotel achieved a stature and importance of its own during the growth of Keighley into a town of substance in the West Riding. Its site close to the hub of Keighley's business, commercial and social life gave it the advantage of being accessible to the people who used the town centre for work and pleasure. If we think that within a stone's throw of this building were the cinemas, the theatre, the shops and the offices, then it is not hard to understand how well the Cavendish once thrived. But change it had to and that applied to all pubs and inns. Over the past 20 years or so many establishments have had to be refashioned to ensure they could satisfy the demand for more pleasant surroundings, for the increase in the number of female customers and for the introduction of new beers and other drinks. Pubs have been expected to serve food as well as drink. They have been forced to change their image and their clientele and their function and have had to endure stiff competition from clubs and from newly built or refurbished hostelries. How well pubs like the Cavendish have moved away from 'men only' atmosphere with simple furniture and selling only 'mild' or 'bitter is for the customer to judge.

Left: A pre-Christmas exhibition of children's literature brought a large crowd of children to the lecture hall in Keighley Library in December 1961. The choice of book by the young man in the duffle coat shows he was, even at that age, determined to get on in the world while no doubt children's librarian, Miss Jean Simpson, is giving those two girls a helping hand in choosing a book to put on their Christmas present list. The parents hovering around would no doubt have benefitted from Miss Simpson's knowledge of the world of books as they were the ones who would wonder what to buy their children. It is interesting to record that the Library's desire to involve children in literature stretched back as far as November 1929 when local Headteachers were invited to nominate 30 of their pupils for one evening to spend the time between 5 and 8pm in the library.

The children had to be 'likely to be the most interested or gain the most benefit', which could not necessarily be the same group of pupils. It was reported that the children were well-behaved and enjoyed the opportunity which otherwise may not have been given. Then the children's favourite books were 'The Cloister and the Hearth', 'The Vicar of Wakefield', 'Lorna Doone' and any book by Robert Louis Stevenson.

Above: An innovation to the children's library in October 1961 was Story Time and here we see the children's librarian, Miss Jean Simpson, on the first evening, reading to the first set of children aged between seven and 10 years. They had been chosen from 10 schools from different parts of the borough and a carefully arranged programme which promised to be educational, instructive and entertaining was on the menu. Interestingly enough the evening began with a piece of music by the British composer, William Coates, followed by the reading of a Scandinavian Folk-tale and a poem by Walter de la Mare. The children were encouraged to talk about what they had heard and were shown new books. That first evening was conducted, as far as the onlookers would allow, in an informal atmosphere in the lecture hall above the children's library. This venture was breaking new ground for the idea that reading books could be entertaining and pleasurable was hard for some people to swallow then. This was the beginning of an age when children's fiction took on a new lease of life and many fine authors began to write books which children, and many a parent. found fascinating and often entrancing. It was, therefore, to Keighley Library's credit that children, albeit a limited few, were given a chance to explore language and story in such an innovative way.

At leisure

Above: This snowy view from Marsh Lane in Oxenhope was taken in February 1955 when the Pennines were once again enduring 'Arctic weather'. The poor fellow out in those conditions deserves all our sympathy. It would not be easy for him having to work in the cold and the snow. Except that to many he and his colleagues may not deserve any sympathy but even condemnation. This man is a reporter for the former Yorkshire Evening News and he is attempting to investigate a local case of Siamese twins being born in the area. Two girls, joined at the head, had been born in Keighley Victoria Hospital at the end of the previous month to the wife of the then manager of Old Oxenhope Farm. Staff at the hospital had been sworn to secrecy but the story did get out three weeks later to the local and then the national press. By then the twins had been moved to London to University College Hospital. The operation to separate them, rated as a two hundred to one chance, was not successful and they died. The case aroused considerable feeling with the hospital authorities accusing the press of causing 'great distress'. The prying or investigative reporting which we expect now and often encourage was not as widespread in those days and this reporter who would claim he was only doing his job. To many people at that time he was a menace.

Right: When you have a new bicycle and you can't stop admiring its three gears and the room for a saddle bag and the pump and you have a puncture repair kit just in case and Fred has sent as usual the old man who sells ice-cream to Raglan Avenue then life can't be bad.

As long as that lady hurries up and makes up her mind. Of course Fred's ices are popular and that is why they are worth waiting for. Didn't Fred get ninety-six marks out of a hundred at the international ice-cream exhibition at Crystal Palace in London this year and say it was all due to a 'secret ingredient'?

Better than last year when he was awarded a Grade A diploma and said that 1936 would be a winning year and he was right. Fred's great. At last year's Keighley gala he threw tubs of ice-cream out to the crowds of spectators from that van with the big artificial cornet stuck in it. I got one and when we were going home we called in his shop on Fell Lane and my mam bought something for tea and some clothes pegs and some washing powder. He's always open.

I had another cornet. Fred's a nice fellow. He said he would take me round his ice cream factory he has just opened in Alice Street as long as I don't tell anyone about that secret ingredient. Wish she would hurry up!

A 1930s view from the Town Hall and across the Town Hall Square with the United Methodist Free Church on Cavendish Street dominating this scene and the whole area. The spire at 125 feet in height was the highest in the town and earned it the then popular local title of Cock Chapel, a sobriquet it retained until its demolition in 1951. It had been closed for worship in 1937 but was re-opened at the beginning of the Second World War as the headquarters of the Keighley Squadron of the Air Defence Corps. Before the War Memorial was erected in 1924 there was just a railed circle of trees in its centre. At least that was a finer sight than previously for at the beginning of the century the square was nothing more than a fenced off Keighley Corporation builder's yard containing, it would appear, every tool and piece of equipment the corporation possessed. The descriptions of it as an 'eyesore' and a 'blot on the landscape' were probably accurate compared to what it did become. Here with every seat full of people taking their ease the square has a dignity of its own befitting its place at the centre of town and it became a centre for meetings and demonstrations throughout the years in war and in peace. It was said every town and city needed a civic focal point and the Town Hall Square certainly was, and is, Keighley's.

Above: A 1960 photograph of the Central milk bar in Bow Street. Today it looks pretty ordinary, nothing really special just a little place to buy a Cadbury's chocolate if you didn't want to go in and if you did you could get a cup of coffee or a milk-shake. But these were the days of change for the young and coffee bars were part of that change.

Coffee, and there were many new ways of serving it like Cappuchino, became a more fashionable drink. New music and new musicians were a increasing focal point of many a young person's life and coffee bars met that head on with juke boxes, even live music - after all was Tommy Steele not 'discovered' singing in a coffee bar? We could listen to Britain's answer to Elvis, Cliff Richard, and did our parents approve?

In our brave hearts in public that did not matter- We stated we were 'BORED' and we began to wear unusual clothes like JEANS as a sign of wanting to be different. There were individual hair styles. We let it grow beyond the short back and sides and even let it hang below our collar. We met in coffee bars and listened to Elvis and eventually the Beatles. We read the 'New Musical Express' and scoured it for news of the Top Twenty as though our livelihood depended on what was number one. We needed to know who was who in the world of music. We asserted our need for more independence in the way we approached our lives - as long as our parents let us.

The struggle to compete with other forms of entertainment in the 1950s proved too much for the Hippodrome and it presented its last show in 1956. It would appear to be appropriate that a local company should have that honour for the musical tradition of the town was so strong. This last show was Keighley Amateur Operatic Society's production of 'Oklahoma', a musical which has endured for years. It is interesting that the theatre world at the time was full, or appeared to be full, of 'angry young men' like John Osborne whose play 'Look Back in Anger' had just opened at the Royal Court theatre in London and sparked off a boom while provincial theatres declined. Efforts to keep the Hippodrome going by Francis Laidler's widow were varied and come to nought. These had included 'girlie' shows and gimmicks like Sandy Strickland, otherwise known as 'Syncopating Sandy', and his successful attempt to break the non-stop piano playing record. He tinkled the ivories for 133 hours commencing on the Monday and finishing, appropriately, on Saturday evening. 20,000 people thought he was worth watching. Apparently, as one report suggested, he must have been pretty close to breaking the non-stop smoking record at the same time if there ever was one and if nothing else Syncopating Sandy was up to date for he began and he ended his marathon performance with 'The Dam Busters March'. No matter what was tried, the theatre finally closed in 1956

Above: The Keighley Queen's Theatre and Opera House, later the Hippodrome, spent five years after its closure as a monument to the town's past. This five storey building, designed by Frank Matcham, architect of many late Edwardian and early Victorian theatres, possessed a large gallery, which could accommodate 400 people, in its pit and orchestra stalls there was seating for 422 and in its circles 257. There were six private boxes, bars on every floor, seven dressing rooms, a fine stage and the splendour of the decor. But it soon became a white elephant, unable to compete with the onset of film and television. For five years it stood idle. There had been no buyers for it, despite a great deal of effort, including a public auction held by Dacre Son and Hartley on 3rd October 1956 trying to persuade would-be impresarios that this was a theatre worth saving. And it was sold to an unknown buyer for £10,000. Nothing happened until 1958 when the council paid £15,000 for it and then a great debate raged as to its future. West Yorkshire Omnibus Company bought it next for the same price and in 1961 it was demolished. Keighley had destroyed one of its old gems and replaced it with a building more in keeping with the needs of the times.

Right: A view of one of Keighley's great buildings, the Queen's Theatre, opened in 1900 on Bow Street and re-named the Hippodrome not long afterwards in 1909 and, in fact, it was known locally by both names for many years afterwards. It was the third theatre to occupy the site since the 1880s. The comparison with the Alhambra Theatre in Bradford is obvious as both had the same impresario, Frank Laidler, who acquired the theatre in 1913. During its 60 years of life it had a chequered history and in its hey day, when many a theatregoer would come straight from work with his sandwiches, before the advent of popular cinema and that bane of live local entertainment the television, the theatre was a very popular music hall and centre of local family entertainment rivalling similar venues in Bradford and Halifax with top names such as Liverpool's Tommy Handley star of radio's 'ITMA', Norman Evans, George Formby, the ukelele man with his often outrageous songs - well,they were at the time - and Rochdale's own Gracie Fields, the centenary of whose birth is being celebrated lavishly this year.The D'Oyley Carte Opera Company performed their Gilbert and Sullivan Operas and repertory theatre companies were frequent visitors with at least five companies having seasons there. The age of variety shows was coming to a close however and the theatre could not rely on touring companies only for its living.

Determination and success for a hundred years

It is exactly 100 years since an enterprising young engineer, Tom Harrison, decided to set up his own business. He found suitable premises that were available for rent in the yard of the Great Northern Railway, acquired a hand cart, and began trading in nuts and bolts. The building occupied a key position near the railway, and as consignments of fasteners arrived by train he was able to pick them up and deliver them to the many engineering companies around Keighley. Tom Harrison carried on his business alone until 1910 when he formed a partnership with Arthur Clough. Two years later, on 24th September 1912, the company was incorporated under the Companies (Consolidation) Act of 1908. A change of premises around about the same time took the business to Park Royd Works in Park Street, which the partners rented from Keighley Corporation. The firm's name was to be linked with the premises for the next 50 years.

The partners erected a small unit adjacent to Park Royd Works to accommodate a small fastener manufacturing operation, and Tom Harrison managed this side of the business while Arthur Clough took control of the merchandising.

An Oldham company, the Oldham Bolt & Nut Works Ltd, went into liquidation in 1912 and Harrison & Clough were quick to recognise its potential. They bought the plant and business and formed the Oldham Bolt & Nut Works (1912) Ltd. Tom Harrison took on the running of the new company while Arthur Clough remained responsible for the merchanting side of the business in Keighley. Communication was much more of a problem in the early years of the 20th Century, a factor that with today's telephone systems, fax facilities, internet connections, fast cars and motorways we tend to forget.

It was the commuting and communication problems that led to the next development when during one frenetic weekend in 1914 the Oldham Company was transferred to Keighley. Tom's son John Harrison retained a vivid memory of that move when in the space of just a couple of days the entire plant relocated to its new site, Riverside Forge, on the banks of the River Worth. The company was renamed the Keighley Bolt & Nut Works Ltd, and both partners took equal shares in both businesses.

Tom Harrison and Arthur Clough had complete confidence in each other; business was good and in 1917, seven years after they first formed their partnership, they made a formal agreement that the partnership would never be dissolved. It was only two years later, however, that Arthur Clough had second thoughts about the arrangement. He asked Tom Harrison to

agree to ending the partnership - a proposal to which Tom took grave exception. A quarrel ensued, with Arthur Clough threatening to start up his own business in competition. In the end a compromise was reached; they each bought the other out and went their separate ways. Tom Harrison retained the manufacturing plant while Arthur Clough took over the merchanting unit retaining the name Harrison & Clough Ltd.

The year 1918 brought an end to the First World War and the demobilisation of troops. A young bookkeeper, Herbert Hutchinson, returned to Keighley after the war only to find that his job in the accounts office of I & I Craven's textile mills was no longer open to him. After an anxious time of unemployment punctuated by the occasional temporary job, Herbert Hutchinson eventually secured a position with Tom Harrison, working as bookkeeper at the Keighley Bolt & Nut Works. Hard times lay ahead, however. The 1920s saw the great depression and unfortunately decline set in at the Keighley Bolt & Nut Works. The company was sold and eventually the merchanting company under William Judson went into competition with Harrison & Clough Ltd. Once more, Herbert Hutchinson was out of work. His new knowledge of the fasteners industry gave him an advantage, however, and he went on to Join Harrison & Clough Ltd, eventually becoming Sales Representative. Around the same time, however, other key members of staff left; taking some of the workforce with him, Charles Greenwood started his own business. John Wilson did the same a few years later.

Right: *The company's premises in Starkie Street - 1962 to 1968.*

More seriously, at the turn of the decade Arthur Clough died, leaving his shares in the company to various family members. William H Smith, who was office manager at the time, was appointed Managing Director, and Herbert Hutchinson also joined the Board. The company was, however, without share-holding directors. A meeting was set up with the shareholders, and it was agreed that controlling interest in Harrison & Clough Ltd should pass to Mr Smith and Mr Hutchinson through the sale of shares to them. Because of his position as Managing Director Mr Smith bought rather more shares than Mr Hutchinson. Upon taking control of the business, they found that the company was in serious financial diffi-culties. They kept going, however, and throughout

World War II there was still a demand for nuts and bolts, though supplies were severely limited. The limited supply situation and the stability in prices gave the company time to evolve in other directions, and a lucrative export trade to India was developed. When peace was finally declared in 1945 lateral thinking took Harrison & Clough into the devel-opment of general engineering merchandising while at the same time still specialising in fasteners.

Further restructuring followed in 1957, once more for financial reasons, and after a brief time of trading as H & C (Keighley) Ltd, on 1st of July 1957 the company was re-registered once more as Harrison & Clough Ltd, again with William Smith as Managing Director

and Herbert Hutchinson as Sales Director. Each held the same joint controlling interest as previously. In February 1962 William Smith died and Herbert Hutchinson invited his son Neville to join the company.

Neville Hutchinson was at that time 27 years old. After having spent ten years in the motor vehicle repair trade, eventually becoming a junior manager, he joined Harrison & Clough Ltd to learn the workings of the company. At the same time Henry Fewster joined the firm directly from Keighley Boys' Grammar School; he was destined to become Executive Sales Manager.

The year 1962 saw many changes in the town of Keighley; in preparation for the redevelopment of the town centre a large number of old properties were demolished. Park Royd Works was earmarked for demolition and Harrison & Clough Ltd were forced to vacate, finding temporary accommodation in Goulbourne Street. Interestingly, the rent for 7,000 square feet of space was just £7.00 per week. At that time there was a total of five bolt and nut merchants in the Keighley area. C Greenwood & Co Ltd, John Wilson (Steel) Ltd and H Cockshott & Co Ltd were the three largest companies. Keighley Bolt & Nut Ltd were the smallest - and Harrison & Clough's position as next to the smallest was a matter of prime concern to Neville Hutchinson.

A new office boy, again a school leaver, joined Harrison & Clough in January 1964. The appointment turned out to be a key event; a successful career lay ahead of David Shaw, who would eventually become General Manager.

The move to Goulbourne Street presented Neville with the ideal opportunity to address their need for expansion. It was obvious to him that a company delivery vehicle was a must. Of prime importance was the fact that customers could be served more quickly and efficiently. Secondly, a vehicle would be invaluable during the move. But the factor that would give them the edge over other bolt and nut merchants was that none of their competitors possessed a delivery vehicle. Accordingly, £654.00 was invested in a Bedford CF dropside truck that was capable of carrying 22.5 cwt (1145 kg).

Neville Hutchinson, now a director, decided that it was time for David to face Goliath. He turned his full attention on bringing Harrison & Clough, a small engineers' merchant whose total staff numbered nine and who had a turnover of £52,000, to a position where they would be able to compete with the larger merchants in the area. When GKN Screws & Fasteners decided to apportion its woodscrew and allied products across a hundred specially picked, nationally appointed wholesalers instead of dealing with individual ironmongers, Neville Hutchinson realised the potential for Harrison & Clough. They had long had a close trading relationship with GKN, which gave them the opportunity to negotiate. The

outcome, after much consultation and deliberation, was that the company was granted Class B distributor status, and was given two years to increase its £8,000 per year spend with GKN to £50,000 per year. It was accomplished within the first twelve months, and GKN acknowledged Harrison & Clough's commitment by offering them a distributorship for their sister company, GKN Bolts & Nuts. These two distributorships opened the doors to every engineering merchants and ironmonger's in the area. Larger distributors in distant cities such as Manchester, Newcastle and Sheffield were unable to deliver to West Yorkshire and North East Lancashire regularly - the country's network of motorway links had yet to be built. Harrison & Clough took over the whole area, establishing a reputation for prompt daily deliveries. The company was now on the up and up, and the workforce was working regular overtime to fulfil all its obligations to customers. By 1968 it had outgrown the temporary premises it had moved into six years previously, and had increased its turnover to almost £208,000.

Further up Goulbourne Street, 16,000 square feet of warehouse and office space became available for sale. Harrison & Clough acquired the premises and made the move, becoming the owners of their own property for the first time.

The company's growth and expansion was, however, becoming more than the traditional 'double entry' bookkeeping system could handle. Roy Ellison, a young man of 19, was another key find. Roy moved into the Accounts Office where his sound knowledge of bookkeeping coupled with his discernment and enthusiasm helped his progression to the eventual position of Executive Accounts Manager.

When Roy moved in, the company's only electronic aid was a Sharp Compet electronic calculator. This was before decimalisation, and invoicing was in pounds, shillings and pence, though the Sharp Compet could only work in decimals. Mental gymnastics were needed on the part of the operator who had to turn traditional currency into its decimal equivalent. Roy Ellison progressively introduced new technology as it became available, purchasing the first NCR Computer in 1978.

The company's larger premises offered the opportunity of further growth, and with that aim in mind Neville Hutchinson was promoted from Joint Managing Director to Managing Director. He developed a dependable system of distribution of GKN products within a 50-mile radius of Keighley.

It was time to develop the business further, and a representative was appointed to take over management of the existing customer base. Henry Fewster's appointment as buyer created an opportunity for Neville Hutchinson to explore new sales

Right: *Harrison & Clough's bulk storage warehouse today.*

territories. With a motorway system that was still in its infancy and the M6 terminating at Lancaster, regular fastener supplies into Cumberland, as the area was known at the time, were irregular, being largely dependent on the size of the load. Harrison & Clough were quick to recognise the opportunity this presented to them, and they offered clients in Cumberland a regular and reliable delivery on the same day every week whatever the volume to be delivered. Customers in Cumberland had never had such a service available to them, and business in the area prospered, making good use of the M6 extensions to Penrith and eventually Carlisle.

The company grew swiftly and by 1972 further advancements were needed. John Dewhirst was recruited from Rycrofts in Bradford. John's background was as an ironmonger, but he had gained a wide experience of fasteners during his time at Rycrofts. He created a Purchasing Office and systems within the company, and Henry Fewster was released to become a representative.

While growth continued, recruiting and keeping reliable staff had become a problem in the early 1970s. An application for a position within the warehouse was received from George McArdle, a 52-year-old warehouse supervisor who had just left one of the larger local engineering companies.

As no formal management structure existed at that time, the three Harrison & Clough directors were responsible for all things, with support from experienced members of staff. Coming from a much larger company, George McArdle stuck out against joining Harrison & Clough as a warehouseman, and even

Left: Today's order assembly warehouse.
Below: The Goulbourne Street premises - 1968 to 1981.

hesitated to accept the newly created position of Warehouse Manager with the much smaller firm. George was given from noon on Saturday until the same time on Monday to make up his mind. His decision to join the company was fortuitous; for the first time there was a manager there to take on the responsibility and control of everything that happened within the warehouse. At the same time a formal management team was created: David Shaw became General Manager, Henry Fewster Sales Manager, Roy Ellison became Accounts Manager and John Dewhirst the Purchasing Manager. The creation of a management team meant that the company could develop further the reliable customer service it took pride in, backed up by an extensive range of stock. Other merchants in the area had by this time ceased to be major competitors. Much larger wholesale distributors from further afield were, however, becoming aware of the swiftly growing GKN distributor in Keighley. Help came from an unexpected quarter....

Dennis Healey, the Keighley-born Labour Chancellor of the Exchequer, had developed policies that encouraged high levels of stock holding, with profitable tax benefits available through annual increases in stock values. Consequently Harrison & Clough found themselves in need of even more warehouse space, and 5,000 square feet of warehousing facilities was rented in Thwaites Village in 1975. Three years later the need for more space was still pressing, and a further 8,000 square feet of space was rented in Eastwood Mills, Aireworth Road in spite of the fact that the property was marked for eventual demolition to make way for the Aire Valley Trunk Road. Holding stock in three separate locations, however, was found to be very inefficient. The search began to find suitable land for the relocation of all three units.

It was found in the form of three acres that were available behind Aireworth Mills, and the first 16,000 square feet of warehouse space was completed by the summer of 1979. Stock was transferred from the two rented warehouses in Thwaites and in Aireworth Road. Construction of a second warehouse and offices then began, and by July 1981 building work was completed. The business was moved from Goulbourne Street to the new site, and the benefits of operating from one position were felt immediately.

The 1980s presented the company with the challenge of worldwide recession. Turnover and profits fell significantly but the firm survived and recovered well.

The granting of distributorships by the GKN Group's fastener manufacturing companies during the 1960s had played a key role in Harrison & Clough's development. GKN now withdrew from the industry, and ironically it was their demise that freed their distributors from the pricing structures and conditions set by GKN, who had controlled the market for more than 80 years. The new freedom of operation enabled the company to offer competitive British made products and to buy and sell at attractive terms. Sales turnover quadrupled and ongoing expansion made it necessary to build a further two warehouses on the Aireworth Road site.

At that time Neville Hutchinson's two sons, Mark and Ian graduated from college and joined the business. After a thorough grounding in the business they went on to join the main board, becoming Operations Director and Sales Director respectively.

Their intention was to continue to develop the company, utilising the challenges of a market place that was changing. It was no longer possible to be competitive by offering British made fasteners or by trying to match the prices offered by competitors on low quality products. The decision was made to continue to offer quality products that were priced accordingly, with the promise of next day delivery from an extensive stock. Relationships were built up with European manufacturers. Mark and Ian visited the Far East in March 1992 to assess quality and price - and the source of some of their competitors' products.

Difficulties lay ahead, however. It was realised that because high levels of effort were being rewarded by low profit levels, the only future in fasteners was to increase market share. A five-year programme of expansion was implemented, and lateral thinking turned the company towards alternative products. Jeff Linley joined the company in November 1994 to form a hand tool division. Its success demanded that higher stock levels were necessary, and 17,000 square feet of new warehouse space was opened on Royd Ings Avenue with the facility to store pallets in 32ft high racking.

The company was developing in other areas, with an extended sales force in Scotland and in the south. A newly-opened distribution depot in Leicester ensured daily delivery to customers as far south as the M25.

In 1995 at the age of 60, Neville Hutchinson gave up his position as Managing Director in favour of his eldest son Mark, who had in 1987 secured BS5750 quality systems recognition for the company and had restructured the entire warehouse storage system. Ian retained his position as Sales Director.

Mark inherited a management team that over the last 30 years had helped to build the company from a small engineers merchant to a leading distributor of fasteners. A Purchasing Manager was added to the team, with specific responsibility for world-wide sourcing, as was an Information Technology manager who would bring the company's ageing systems into the world of the latest computing systems.

From the small beginnings 100 years ago, when Tom Harrison started his one-man business in the station yard, the company had become one of the nation's major wholesalers of Fasteners, Fixings and Hand Tools. Led by a management team who are blessed with a combination of youthful enthusiasm, experience and professionalism, Harrison & Clough Ltd eagerly looks forward to the opportunities which await after their Centenary celebrations in 1999.

Below: *The Leicester based transport fleet.*
Bottom: *The present day premises on Aireworth Road.*

Expansion and development of the company, whose staff today numbers 225, continued; the sales team was strengthened in the south, both for fasteners and for hand tools; 'own branding' of many fastener lines for the merchant trade was introduced, and a second distribution depot was opened in Reading. A professionally qualified Financial Manager was appointed in February 1998. In October of the same year the Royd Ings Avenue development was completed.

Bird's eye view

The streets around East Parade and Coney Lane were adapted to accommodate Worth Way, which encircles the Greengate area of the town

It is estimated that two thirds of Keighley as shown in this photograph will in the next thirty years or so disappear or be radically altered. North Street runs down the left hand side with St Anne's Church and School near its junction with Spring Gardens Lane. Opposite is the Picture House, cum Essoldo, now restored to its former name and thankfully showing films again. Nearly all the way down this street will remain untouched although buildings like the Devonshire Street Congregational Chapel will disappear. The part that will 'suffer' is the centre and it would be interesting to try to recall what is here now and what will replace it. The railway goods yard behind Cavendish Street will be developed, as will the other side around Fleece Mills and the area above it. At the bottom of Alice Street, opposite the timber yard with its Dutch Barn shape, will be home to Peter Black's new factory. Between the Parish Church and Coney Lane is here Keighley's market area and behind the Church is Hattersley's foundry, both to undergo radical change. The old Fire Station at Low Bridge, subject to almost a never-ending discussion as to its suitability, will remain near the gas holder until the late 1960s when a new one beyond the railway station will replace it. The streets around East Parade and Coney Lane will be adapted to accommodate Worth Way, which will almost encircle the Greengate area of the town. Keighley here is not ready for change yet for in 1938 there are other matters to consider.

Left: Keighley in 1948 shows the Mechanics Institute in its full glory on North Street and next to it on Cavendish Street the Cock Chapel of the United Methodist Free Church, Across the road from the Mechanics Institute stands the Regent Cinema but like the Ritz is no longer used for showing films but for something else. Along North Street where the original Mechanics Institute is here a bank, is the Town Hall and War Memorial while the bus station, smaller than today,cuts a diagonal behind them. The Co-operative buildings on Hanover Street and Brunswick Street, including its own dairy, and the famous Mosley's fish and chip shop will give way to the Airedale Centre as, of course, will other Keighley shops and offices. The railway goods yard behind Cavendish Street, the site of the first railway station, will remain for a few more years until the commercial demands of the late twentieth century will force change to that area and to parts of the other side of that street. The railway station on Bradford Road was opened in 1883 to replace the original. The industrial complexes of Dalton Lane lead off Bradford Road and we follow that road to Keighley's heritage, Victoria Park, subject of a furious debate in the late 1980s as to whether a school should be built on the land. The park and the surrounding area have a tranquil air to them here. The leisure centre and the new roads are yet to come, however.

Above: A pre-war view of the town which should bring back memories of what Keighley was before the redevelopment of the mid 1960s took place. What is left today? North Street, then matching the elegance of Cavendish Street, still has the Town Hall and its open Square and War Memorial. There is still the Library and the Temperance Hall, the former retaining its original function, the latter not. At the other end of the street where it meets Low Street and High Street stands the Cross, the old centre of the town in the shadow of the Parish Church. Many of the streets here retain their 'shape' later but changes there are to come. The small bus station will eventually undergo two face lifts. The Mechanics Institute will survive until fate takes a hand. The nearby Queens Theatre, under the guiding hand of Francis Laidler, is at the peak of its popularity but will eventually run out of steam and succumb to the demands of modern times. The areas on either side of Low Street will be re-developed with the market area a feature of the town since the last century completely revamped. The Congregational chapels, Upper Green and Devonshire Street, are prominent here and will serve their communities until well after the war as will Temple Street Weslyan Chapel and Sunday School. At the bottom of West Lane is the National School and the bus garages dominate Keighley's French connection, Suresnes Road.

Below: The Airedale Centre is almost complete in this June 1967 view of the town. The ramp to take cars from Hanover Street to the multi storey car park is in place and this park will certainly ease the traffic problems of the town centre. The new bus station, adjoining the centre, has yet to be completed and the market area to the rear of Low Street still awaits the developers. North Street cuts its way across the top part of the photograph and at its junction with Cavendish Street work on the Technical College extension is in full swing with the disappearance of the Cock Chapel and the Municipal Hall having left gaps in the list of Keighley's old landmarks. Across the road are the traditional buildings or the town, the Temperance Hall with its unique weather vane, the grand Library and the businesses that feature so strongly in that area. The Police Station has been extended and on the opposite side the original Mechanics Institute is soon to be demolished. Behind North Street the new Devonshire House has replaced the old Congregational Chapel. To its right is the Scott Street car park. The sweep of the elegant Cavendish Street stops at the Victoria Hotel at its junction with East Parade. Before we reach the approach to the car park, another long standing feature of the town, the Fleece Mills complex of William Sugden Ltd meets the eye. A photograph of a Keighley in the process of change.

Right: A post 1968 view of the town, with the War Memorial in the Town Hall Square standing out in the centre. The new Keighley Technical College is half way to completion and the other developments around the town centre are almost in place. Morrison's new store is the first to be built outside Bradford and will become part of the area to include the new market.

The Police Station on North Street and the Magistrates Courts have been extended. Yorkshire Bank has new premises on the opposite side of the road to the original one and the chimney of the swimming baths rises high behind the Library. Albert Street Baptist Chapel and Scott Street car park complete this end of the photograph while over the road on Alice Street stands the Ritz Cinema, the last and most spacious to be built in the town. It could seat fifteen hundred and boasted a three manual electric organ and a one hundred seater cafe. At the top of the street the offices of the Keighley News can just be made out.

The multi storey car park, serving the shoppers who can now use the Airedale Centre, stands on the site of the old Queens Theatre. On the far side of the centre is Low Street, now closed to through traffic. Worth Way is not there just yet. The railway line leading up the Worth Valley has just been re-opened after years of waiting. Keighley has fought a battle and won here.

Around the town centre

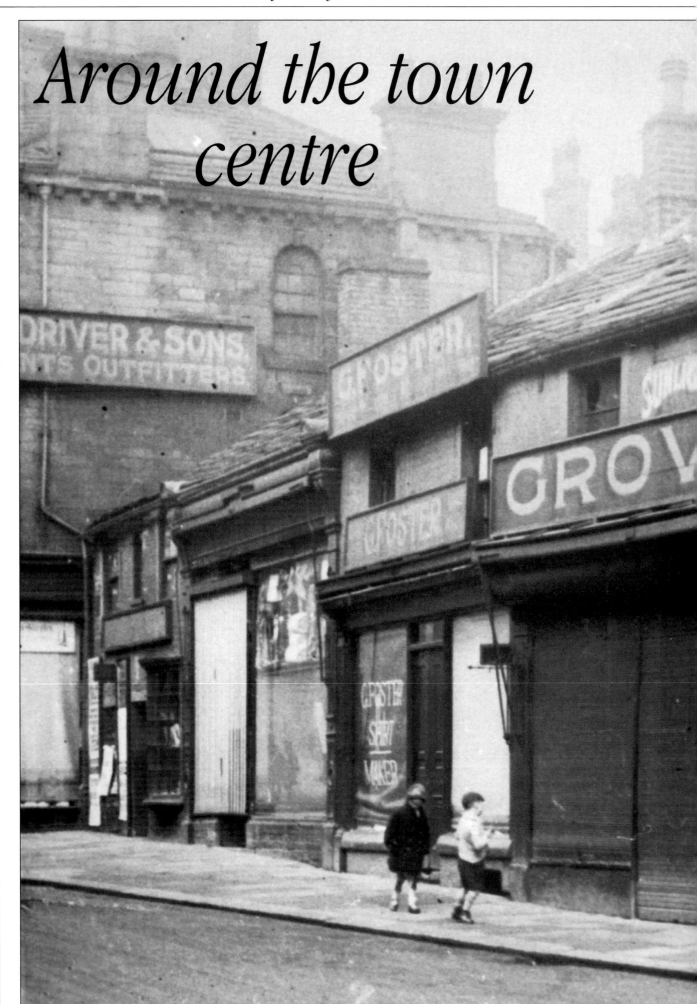

Groves at the junction of Low Street and Cooke Lane was interesting in that it was one of the oldest shops in Keighley and that it claimed to offer a truly personal service. It must have been old for it had that 'Ye Olde Shoppe' sign outside 45 years at least before this view. The two little boys passing Fosters, the shirt makers, seem to be heading for the shop but they are going to be disappointed. There does not appear to be anything behind the windows for them to stick their noses up against - they were long boarded up. Perhaps they have come to remind themselves of the fascination of Cadbury's Cocoa or a cup of hot Oxo or Bovril. 'Good for your chest' a granny would advise.

The old proprietor of the shop, James Groves, is well remembered for his patriotic gesture when he presented every soldier going off to the Boer War with a bar of soap, no doubt well appreciated at the time. Little was he to know that years later his shop would be the site of Boots the Chemist. They, however, had no use for dingy and dark little shops and two extra storeys were soon added.

Above: The window boxes outside
Gillian Whittaker's hairdressing salon
provide a sharp contrast to what her
customers will have seen as they looked
across the road at the waste land that
was Low Street at its junction with East
Parade and Coney Lane in April 1969.
Keighley is still in the developers' grip.
Wild's has lost one branch of its baking
and confectionery business. Curry's has
gone to the new Queensway and Singer
the sewing machine shop will re-locate
to Church Street. The plan to demolish
this side of the street had been well
known for some years and what was to
replace them were the new Worth Way
and the offices of the Department of
Social Security. This is about the ninth
year of the move to re-vitalise
Keighley's centre so that it can cope
with the demands of the increase in
traffic and the change in people's
shopping habits and general life styles.
Life appears to go on in the Co-op's
decorating branch, in L&C Weatherwear
and Rubber shop and in Bacon and
Coates but where are the shoppers? The
effect of having such a long drawn out
operation as this was probably, in retrospect, demoralising for shop owners
and confusing for their customers. It
could well have been some time before
those businesses at the tail-end of this
plan could say it was all worth it.

Right: This gentleman in Brunswick
Street appears to be checking his change
or counting how much he has left as he
contemplates possibly which of the many
premises belonging to Keighley
Industrial Co-operative Society he should
enter. He has a large choice in November
1960. The Co-op also played an
important role in the cultural life of its
members. Here in Brunswick Street were
once the Co-operative Assembly Rooms
and regular concerts were given and to a
town with such a rich musical tradition
as Keighley's they were well received.
There was also the Keighley Co-operative
Society's Men's Guild with weekly
meetings and discussions which were
very much in line with the Society's traditions. Subjects for discussion included
'Brotherhood - the Need of the Age', ' Sir
Thomas More's Utopia', 'The Productive
Side of the Co-operative Movement' and
'How to Keep Well'. It held Co-operative
Day for the elder members of the society
and in one year 1500 people were enter-
tained to tea and entertainment in halls
throughout the area. That evening's
entertainment of a concert and film was
held in the Municipal Hall with a queue
forming one and a half hours before it
was due to start and even then a 100
were turned away. At the end each guest
was presented with a gift parcel from the
Middleton Jam Factory.

ESTD 1860

Church Green. known officially as Church Street, has in 1966 changed very little over the past sixty or seventy years as we view it from the Parish Church. The pinnacles are its great landmark for this is the crescent which was widened in 1890 by Alderman Richard Longden Hattersley as a frontage to his foundry and to accommodate the Conservative Club as well as shops and houses. It was regarded then as being an important innovation in the area of street improvement. The Keighley side of the Hattersley story began in 1800 when premises in South Street were opened to produce spindles, rollers and spares for the growing textile trade. Soon the business was manufacturing powered looms for weaving worsted cloth. Progress through the nineteenth century was unhin-

dered and by 1914 Hattersley's employed over 1,000 workers. The new premises bought at Greengate became its permanent home and there it remains today only operating rather differently to when it was 'at its peak'. The Church Green area was regarded as the old heart of the town. To widen it, as Hattersley did, enhanced its status and was the forerunner of other road improvement schemes in the town. North Street, the important traditional route north to Skipton and Kendal, was next. Like Church Green its new width gave it an air of spaciousness, albeit on a larger scale, and both streets could not fail to impress any visitor to the town.

This is 1966, however, and a full car park on Bridge Street brings us back to the reality of the 1960s.

Above: The buildings at the junction of Cooke Lane and Bow Street in July 1966 look serene enough obviously unaware of their future as outlined by the planners. The street cleaner is 'on his beat' and the only slight hint all is not as it should be is that Johnson and Errick's shop is now in the temporary hands of Oxfam. To its left is the famous bonded warehouse of E T Wall Ltd whose shop was situated on Hanover Street. The heavily barred windows can just be made out and the store could only be entered in the presence of member of the Customs and Excise who had the only key to the lock. This warehouse was known officially as No.1 Duty Free Warehouse and the reason for all this security were the fine Italian wines Walls imported and their own brand of rum which needed seven years to mature. Behind the lamp standard and appropriately, or otherwise, next to the spirit store stands the Salvation Army Citadel. Its call for temperance stands squarely against its spirited neighbour. In today's times health food stores abound and newspapers and magazines seem to be as concerned with our well being as much as what we wear. The sight of the health food store here would be somewhat unusual over thirty years ago. The growth in the fast food industry is to be matched by the move towards healthy eating, the avoidance of highly processed foods and those containing additives. Thus grew the wholefood industry to cater for these tastes and the health stores were welcome major contributors towards a growing movement.

Top: The crane lurking at the meeting of Cooke Lane, Bow Street and Lawkholme Crescent is waiting to pounce dispelling any air of permanence about the area. The flag over the Town Hall casts an almost magisterial eye over the Salvation Army Citadel, the bonded warehouse and the Post Office, whose building carries an air of authority about it which commands in 1966 a respect for its function and its history. Today it appears to be no more than a very useful counter service without the status it once possessed. The Ramsbottom's van, parked on Cooke Lane, is not far from the shop in Bow Street. Where other small family businesses didn't succeed in the 'consumer' war of the 1960s, Ramsbottom's did. It had been part of the Keighley shopping scene since 1924 and prided itself on its slogan 'The Complete Electricians'. It was not afraid to try new innovations such as Radio Rental and Radio Relay or open a coffee bar and to be aware of the revolution in the musical tastes of the young. What could have been more trendy than to go in 1956 to Ramsbottom's new record showroom 'the only music store in town fitted with a soundproof audition room'? There you could listen to the recently discovered Elvis Presley's hit 'Heartbreak Hotel' or his new releases, 'Hound Dog' and the smoochy 'Love me Tender' with your friends squeezed in the booths with only one pair of earphones between you. Happy days!

Another view along Hanover Street showing the Keighley Co-operative building which dates back to 1860. It would be one of the first towns in the area to follow the lead of the Rochdale Pioneers in 1844 and set up their own business in line with the famous Rochdale principles of open membership, democratic control and political and religious neutrality, easy to assimilate in this age but not so easy in the middle of the nineteenth century. The Co-op had premises in Brunswick Street and Low Street as well as in Hanover Street. The offices were located in Brunswick Street together with a range of shops ranging from household goods, clothing, food, a dairy in Hanover Street and various other services which set the Co-op apart from other businesses. Each customer would be given the opportunity to become a member, to have their own Co-op number which was recited each time a purchase was made, ready for that day when the Co-op announced its dividend to its customes or shareholders and payment was made on dividend or 'divvy' day.The range of services increased from insurance, to travel, to funerals and at the height of their popularity after the war the Industrial Co-operative Societies like Keighley's were an integral part of people's lives until other retail establishments were set up to compete for people's loyalty and increased spending power.

Right: It is difficult to imagine a time when land in the centre of town could be turned over to temporary car parking seemingly very easily while the whole district was undergoing massive redevelopment. Little is known about the reason that this picture was taken, but it is likely that a far-sighted photographer intended to record the view for *the record*. Advertising boards indicate the location of the Keighley Brake Service which apparently also supplied Crompton batteries. the picture dates from the early 1960s and features several interesting vehicles. Not least of these is the Ford Anglia estate car. The most popular colour of these was *turquoise* and they represented the first serious competition for the even more popular Morris Travellers of the day.

Below: A very uneven pavement lined the shop windows along this quiet, cobbled street, complete with ancient gas-lamp which was still in working order despite being well over 60 years old. Some of the shops in this scene will be familiar to people who

remember 'old Keighley.' Winstons was a favourite with fashion-conscious ladies, with spacious premises offering outfits suitable for every occasion. Hargreaves stood next door. In the distance several properties had already been pulled down in the late 1950s. This created a patch of open ground which followed the normal course of events by becoming a 'temporary' car park. In the days featured here 'temporary' often meant as long as a decade before a new property was constructed. The demolition had exposed a broad gable end on the adjacent building which, according to the sign positioned upon it, was the home of J. Wright's Auto-Electrical business. Some of the motors on the temporary car park may have been occasional customers. The Morris Minors, Hillman Minx and ubiquitous Austin A35's which were best sellers of their day and therefore common sights on local roads. Slightly less common was an early Reliant Regal three-wheeler which owed its limited popularity to the fact that holders of motorbike licences could drive them legally.

Left: This is an aerial view from the Parish Church of the south end of the town towards West Lane. At the front of the photograph is the rear of Church Green and we look towards High Street, one of the town's oldest streets, before it meets West Lane, Turkey Street and Oakworth Road. Turkey Street here in 1966 with the sign for Woodbine cigarettes was very close to demolition. Just before Oakworth Road starts to climb, that flat part to the left was for some reason known as New Road. Behind High Street are the flat roofs of the corporation bus garages on Suresne Road, named after a district of Paris with which Keighley had a worker exchange in the early 1900s. This was part of the national efforts to bring about an 'entente cordiale' between this country and France in order that the people of both countries would have a better understanding of each other's way of life, amongst other things. On High Street one recognisable building is the Grapes public house which has managed to survive better than the Ship Inn at the bottom of West Lane which was demolished in 1969 after its owners Bentley Yorkshire Breweries Ltd let its licence lapse and the popular pub had the indignity of having its frontage shored up with timber.

Below: This is a November 1960 view of the east side of Coney Lane near the junction with East Parade looking towards Low Street. Very little appears to have changed over the years across the road unless a closer inspection is needed. The Electricity Showrooms in Coney Lane were once described as a 'paragon of tasteful design', by whom it is not recorded, but in the pre-world war style of the 1920s and 1930s it would have its own elegance. It did manage to win first prize in the competition organised by the Keighley Chamber of Trade for the best decorated exterior for the Coronation of Edward 8th in 1937 so it was obviously a highly regarded building. It has now gone and to replace it is a building best described as functional and serving its purpose at the time but not in keeping with the rest of the old structures. Of the other shops we can see here only Bacon and Coates remains. The Royal Arcade erected in 1899 then led to Butterfields and was an extremely popular part of the town's trade but today it appears forlorn and unwanted. This is a pity for surely there is a need for this kind of area if the town wants to develop as well as retaining what was traditional and useful.

Below: A 1962 photograph with 1962 prices in Maypole. If you want to take up their offer of butter, the choice will be have to be by preference or in the eating but not in the price as they all cost the same at 3s.3d or today's price of 17 pence per pound while today it is approximately £2! A giant Persil today is a few hundred per cent more expensive. Maypole was regarded as one of the more economical stores at which to shop but even this company had begun to find life difficult for the competition with its rivals had become too fierce. So, although they retained their names and their individual shop fronts, Maypole, Lipton, Home and Colonial and lesser names like Broughs and Meadow did what other companies in other businesses did and become one company called the Home and Colonial Group. The impact of national chains was beginning to tell but local shops fought on, although at this time on the north side of Low Street between Hanover Street and Coiney Lane it must have been early closing day or why is the jewellers, Barwick and Haggas closed at 3.40 p.m.? At least the quiet time gives that gentleman chance to look in Walco's at the Tuf shoes which he might need for Winter if the previous Winter's weather was anything to go by.

Left: Another quiet day on Low Street as we look down towards the Market Street area on the right of the photo-graph. The familiar line of shops would give an air of permanence to the street and the traffic problems which beset towns appear to be non-existent here. Below Stylo is Redmans the 'Good Bacon' shop. It always appeared to have on its display shelves and counters enough bacon to feed an army for it never seemed to be short of any cut.

Next to Redmans is the furnishers, Jays, advertising as well as their furniture their 'easy terms' as the credit and consumer boom of the 1960s took off. Items which are taken for granted in homes today were added to the family's inventory. In the same way as dish washers, microwave ovens, compact disc players and home computers have became 'growth areas' in the 1990s, so colour televisions, refriger-ators, video-recorders and deep freezers were just some of the items of that decade and the hire-purchase industry expanded at a tremendous rate. The number of people taking foreign holidays increased rapidly and travel agents like Althams began to become a common fixture on the high streets of every town.

Another reminder of what was. The Low Street in 1962 initially appears little differently in certain aspects to that of today at least from the photograph. A roll-call of the shops will bring back a memory or two as we start from East Parade, Coney Lane junction and work our way up the incline following British Railway's three wheeler. First of all it is a one way street even in those days which shows how busy or narrow or both the street was. This branch of Keighley Co-op, the home decor side of the business has a sale on. Below the crown of the aptly named Crown buildings is the ladies' hair stylist of Gillian Whittaker. At this time the street is a mixture of local shops like Wild's with the established nationals like Freeman Hardy and Willis who had shod the nation for years or John Collier, 'the Window to Watch', and Currys Electricals and Singer sewing machine shop. Because they had been part of every town scene for many years they were regarded as trustworthy locals. Soon there will be big changes in this area but Low Street does survive. The Co-op has retained its position but others moved indoors to the new centre or left town or in the case if L & C Rubber Company to we know not where. So today's first glance does not tell the whole story and compared it to nearly 40 years ago, Low Street has lost that vitality so evident in this photograph.

Melias advertises its Provisions which gave it a superior sounding air and the gentleman about to load his car is owning type of car which will become very popular in the next few years The growth in the number and makes of the saloons, the hatchbacks and the estate cars soon will offer a greater variety of choice to the motorist. The window shopper at the Famous Army Stores may well be tempted by the offer of a free pair of jeans or overalls for every twenty-fifth customer, unless he is counting the number and lying in wait! Today jeans are a common item in almost everyone's wardrobe and it is not 'do you own a pair? but 'how many and what make?' But the sixties was the beginning of the triumph of denim jeans. Originally a tough working garment from North America they were at first imported under the original brand name of 'Levis' and, like the mini skirt for the fashion conscious miss at the time, they became a standard part of the young's 'national uniform'. Many a young man would stand proudly in front of his mirror with his first pair of Levis or Wranglers, for other manufacturers began to copy, and feel he was the 'bee's knees' and then think how even more fashionable he would be in a hooded anorak, better than the duffel coat he had for school last year.

and the Co-op had been completed. The plan to pedestrianise Low Street is still to come about and the street here has a lop-sided look - busy on one side, bereft on the other. It is this side of the street that is now waiting its turn for the bulldozer and the crane.

Top: A delightfully nostalgic scene dating from 1962 shows an uncharacteristically quiet Lawkholme Crescent. An elderly man can be seen taking his small dog for a walk around the town, possibly on an early morning shopping trip intended to collect a few 'essentials' before the rush. Ryley & Sons stationers might have had something of interest for the man in their packed windows. Above Keighley's best-known suppliers of school and office requisites was a dental practice. In the era featured here a trip to the dentist would have been a fearsome experience. Not that there was anything wrong with the dentists of the day; like so many aspects of health and life in general, we have moved on since the time when people would pay for their offspring to have false teeth fitted as a twenty-first birthday present! By the time this photo-graph was taken most of the buildings shown here had been earmarked for demolition. This was the dawn of Keighley's retailing revolution, a time which would see the landscape of the centre of town change forever.

Above: Times have moved on for Low Street in 1968 and the shells of that once were busy thriving shops look in a sorry state. Maxwells at the corner with Park Street has stopped selling its gowns and Cavendish on the other corner at Green Street, its furniture. The Co-op has gone elsewhere but Wiseman and Winston, above Jerry's Competitive Price Store, have also appeared to have sold their last gown on this street. The plan to re-develop the centre as outlined by the developers was to be put into operation in stages so for shopkeepers, shoppers and motorists Keighley seemed to be for a decade constantly rebuilding. Low Street, Adelaide Street, Queen Street, Bow Street, Cooke Lane and Hanover Street were part of the first package of clearance between 1960 and 1965 and between 1966 and 1971 property between Cavendish Street and Bow Street was next on the list. By 1968 the first phase had been completed and the re-location of shops like Woolworths, Boots

One of the more famous buildings in Keighley dominated the area for many years as we look across the Bridge Street car park in July 1960. The Upper Green Congregational Chapel, which opened in 1824 as the town's independent place of worship, could seat four hundred and fifty worshippers and was used also for meetings of the Temperance Society, the Glory Band, Penny Readings and public debates before it reverted solely to Congregational worship. The Chapel was demolished in 1964. Across High Street behind Lord's furnishers is the Temple Street Weslyan Methodist Chapel, opened in 1864, and still standing on this narrow cobbled street. It could seat sixteen hundred people. Directly behind the Chapel is the famous Clock Tower of the Keighley Mechanics Institute

on North Street, shortly to meet its end by demolition after a fire. Rivock Edge, towards Ilkley Moor, makes a perfect backdrop to this picture and below we can see the community of Riddlesden. The open area where High Street meets Bridge Street gives a good view of the shops which served the area for some time. Lord's furnishing shop on the corner of Chapel Lane dominated the street because of its size only while Morley's also was in the same trade. The tradition of selling pram and babywear was carried on by Wilson's and on the corner is the spacious Albert Hotel. The roundabout once had a useful purpose apart from traffic control. In the middle is the entrance to a war time air-raid shelter. The line of shops to Church Street ends at Hobson's woolshop on the corner.

Below: The first moves to provide a new site for the Yorkshire Bank began in the latter part of 1965 when Vickers drapers on North Street was demolished. The intention was that the whole of this block should disappear which meant the end of Elizabeth's ladies' fashions. The planners did not reckon on the dentist who practised above that particular concern being somewhat of an expert in planning law. He successfully objected to the plans and he and Elizabeth stayed put for a few more years. The part of that block that appears slightly out if character with the rest were once the offices, until it went out of business in 1911, of the Keighley Herald. North Street seemed then, as it does today, to be thickly populated by banks although the choice is narrower today due to mergers and closures. Banks like the Provincial, the Craven, the District and the Westminster have all gone down that road. The atmosphere has altered a great deal, too. Banks do not possess that awe they had for so long when they almost had a cathedral-like air to them; everyone seemed to talk in whispers as though finance was sacred. Compare that to the more informal hustle and bustle of today's financial institutions as the competition for our custom and our money is wider as a different other businesses have joined in.

Left: The lady on the edge of the pavement seems to want to cross Low Street; there can be no traffic coming down this one way street so her indecision must be regarding something else. Perhaps it is a surprise that both shops belonging to Timothy Whites were still open for all else appears forsaken. Timothy Whites, and at one time & Taylors, had long been regarded as Boots' only serious competitor but it appeared to be always one step behind. Like Boots it became more than a chemist shop and like Boots it diversified into things like houseware products. In the end it succumbed and was absorbed by its rival. Despite the chaos all around them both shops, the Chemist and the Houseware department on the corner of Park Street are trying to give an air of 'business as usual' but the demolition sign outside the old Co-op does not encourage the shopper. It looks like a warning to the chemist shop as well being as a safety announcement to the busy shoppers on the other side of Low Street. The area below Park Street which includes Curtess Shoes has still some life in it and there is a property for sale.

That will remain waiting for refurbishment while the top part waits for the coming of a new market area.

This junction where Low Street, North Street, High Street and Church Green traditionally marked the centre of the town or the parish of Keighley. The parish boundary was marked as being within one mile radius of the cross sited at the end of Church Green outside the old Devonshire Arms and this, the adjacent parish church and the market were for several generations regarded as the fulcrum of the town. The market had stood on Church Green from 1833 until 1971 when one of the last pieces of the town's re-development jigsaw was put into place and the whole market area altered in style and character. Even the Devonshire Arms had its name changed to the 'Grinning Rat' which on first impression is not a wholesome name for a place of refreshment but it does have a tradition behind it. The original pub with that name, the Queen's Arms, had been known by that for many years but was demolished in 1966. When the Devonshire Arms was re-opened in 1987, its name became the Grinning Rat. Why Grinning Rat? Two theories. One is that a touring theatre company performed a play of that name in the original pub. The other is that a one-time landlord who was in debt faced the bailiffs with a shotgun and leered at them from the windows like a grinning rat. It is thought the latter story is fiction.

Two contrasting Keighley businesses here yet each in some way played an important part in the shopping life of the town. At the end of the last century local authorities were given the power to create municipally owned gas supplies and in 1902 these gas offices were built in Cooke Lane. After the supply of gas was nationalised by the post-war Labour Government, the responsibility passed in this part of the country to the North Eastern Gas Board which, of course, took over the old building. A sale of cookers and gas fires is being held on this sunny Spring day in 1966 as the competition to sell such appliances becomes more fierce. Direct Discounts did not need a sale for it boasted it could not sell anything more cheaply and the shopper could not buy locally any item more cheaply. This is a practice which has become a popular selling point by retailers over the past few years. The Direct called itself a 'Furniture Supermarket' and a 'Walk Round Store'. This would have been something of a novelty in the 1960s but with there being plenty of potential customers out there, shops did not want to miss any opportunity to bring them in to spend their money. Items once considered a luxury were now in popular demand. The number of labour saving devices in the home increased and so released women - and men - from many domestic chores. A typical example was the sudden spurt at the time in the number of families owning a washing machine, hence the sale in the gas board showrooms.

Right: One of the streets 'hardest hit' by the town's re-development programme was Hanover Street, at one time a very busy thoroughfare with a variety of local businesses like the wine merchants, E.T.Walls, estab-

Below: A far view of the Mechanics Institute and North Street from Church Green in February 1966 with the gentleman on the corner looking rather bemused probably at having his photograph taken. Hofmann's was one of three or four

lished in 1823, Naylors Brass Foundry, the Gardeners Arms and the Wellington which is reputed to have had in the 1930s a 'ladies only' bar.

This October 1962 photograph shows the bit of the street from the Gardeners Arms to its junction with Low Street and East Parade that will survive.

What will remain is what the planners promised. The Co-op will have its electrical store and restaurant beyond the entrance to the roof top car park and the Airedale Centre on the other side of the road will be free from the unpleasantness of modern traffic.

Wide, modern walkways will replace the narrow congested streets and the multi storey car park with that ramp leading from Hanover Street will ensure that shoppers can park a short way from the shops.

In this area there will be the discreet efficient loading areas on a different level to the pedestrian area so the delivery vans will not cause the congestion that they do in 1962. There will be shrubs and flower beds to take away the clinical look of many other town centre devel-opments and the space and cleanliness so important will be there for all to experience.

butchers of German extraction who came to the town before the First World War and had to endure a great deal of anti-German feeling in 1914. The Kings Arms built in 1742 was once an old coaching inn which would be a stopping and stabling place for coaches bound for Halifax, Bradford and Leeds. For some time it was the headquarters of Keighley Rugby League Club and acted as changing rooms for players and officials. The journey to and from the Lawkholme Lane Ground was made in a wagonnette. The inn would have been a very interesting place should the home team ever had lost by a disputed try in the last minute. The club had acquired the ground in 1885 when it amalgamated with the next door Cricket Club and has remained there. In those early days spectators stood out in the open, the grandstand being wagons brought in to give some a better view. Highlight of the pre-war years was the appearance at Wembley in 1937 when the club was defeated by Widnes 18 points to 5. The club has had a well-chronicled recent history as it, and many other clubs also, try to come to terms with the demands of the modern era and the vagaries of the game's administrators.

Above: The Parish Church provides the backdrop as we look up Church Street, or Church Green, or Hattersley Crescent. Hattersley's pinnacles, which were the street's trademark, look down and across the curve of shops on a wet Saturday afternoon in July 1968 as the few shoppers make up their minds which of the long established shops to visit this time. The traffic problem of car parking here never goes away although the one-way system has eased it somewhat. Some of the cars themselves give the street an air of opulence although the shopkeepers would claim they belonged to the customers and were not theirs. What this street did have among the traders was an air of permanence as many remained here for some time and it helped establish a sense of loyalty to each other and among their customers. In fact Jewitt's the herbalist and its proprietor, Mr Broadbent, are still in business after more than forty years on the street. Other shops who were a feature the street for some years were Barry Robinson's fish and fruit store, Gallon's, the grocers, and Whitehead's leather shop whose goods were locally made at the shop's tannery on Halifax Road. Other names that were synonymous with that street included Woodhouse Furniture, the bakers, Crabtree, and Wikinson's pet store, Lent's, another furnisher and the shops on the corner for all to see Hobson's and Sugden's. Where are they all now?

Above right: What a bleak picture! There is snow on the car inexplicably parked on the pavement where the long distance bus would once take people to Birmingham and the less harsh climes of Devon and Cornwall. There is

snow on the roofs of the shops and what is left of the other businesses as the re-development gnaws its way into Bow Street. It is a picture of devastation and the lady gazing in to Hobson's store must wonder at it all. The little consolation to be gained in April 1968 is that it will soon be Summer and it will not be long before the end of the seemingly endless noise and disruption if the planners' and developers' promises are kept. That is of scant consolation to the lady scurrying across the road as she is faced with the sight of empty shops, rubble on the pavement and now to cap it all it has snowed. Promises are all right but she has to live and work and shop amongst this. The effect on business for those at the end of the development queue must have been hardest to bear. All that long and slow waiting for the death sentence and then it comes. A notice of closure, getting rid of stock, problems with staff futures, your own future and livelihood. Then it is time to move out and the demolition squad to move in. Or that is how it must have felt. Buildings whose design are in keeping with Keighley's.

A mother has left her push chair outside Driver's Milk Bar on Lawkholme Crescent on this bright and fine February day in 1968. Milk and coffee bars continued to be popular meeting places for teenagers and those still young at heart. Outside is the car which has stood the test of generations and defied the prognostication of at least one of its makers that it would not sell - the Morris 1000. To take advantage of the popularity of Driver's, next door but one up the narrow staircase is the Palace Coffee Bar. The two ladies looking in the window of Speak's must be deciding on what kind of outdoor clothing to buy or maybe they are just window shopping or even wondering if they dare visit ABT Commission agents situated above the Milk Bar. Nestled between the Ford Anglia and the A40 Van in front of the Lakeland Laundry shop is a Lambretta Italian scooter, with its extra seat for a passenger at the rear. The scooter was popular with 'Mods' as opposed to the leather clad motor bike riding 'Rockers' of the day. This part of Lawkholme Crescent managed to avoid the pile driver and the crane and shops like Speaks and Driver's remained in business for the next few years - in fact Speak's survives today and extended its premises nearly twenty years ago to include Driver's so retaining its long standing commitment to the town. The distinctive frontage of the Halifax Building Society at the corner of Cavendish Street stands out here and it is a pity that the building appears unwanted today. However, what can be gleaned from this photograph is that tradition does take some beating.

On the move

Below: A Cedes Stoll trolley bus straddles the old tram lines at the junction of North Street and Low Street in 1921.This splendid example was the number 58, with a greater flexibility than earlier models given to it by converting to front wheel drive. It was claimed that would give greater manoeuvrability in increasingly heavy traffic but nothing was said about passenger comfort. Tramlines had been laid down in 1904 after horse drawn trams had been discontinued but even though there was a tramways system it was not until 1913 the corporation pioneered the the use of trackless cars to the outskirts of the town. The last journey made by a tram was in 1924 to Utley to the Roebuck Inn, which had served as a terminus even in the horse-drawn days.

The electric tram system had been heralded in Keighley in great style with ceremonies and inspections and visits and wonder. Each tram bore proudly the words 'Keighley Corporation Tramways' on its green and crimson livery. But its track was inflexible and expensive to maintain and its fixed routes, although economic, were limited to certain 'narrow' areas of the town.

What it did mean for the town was it had to tear up the tram tracks and re-surface the roads. Skipton Road was a typical example where the road was reduced to half its normal width during the repairs and the erection of trolley standards. The triumph of the electric tram had been short-lived.

Right (both pictures): Standing proudly at the rear of this 'Straker' double decker trolley bus in 1925 is its conductor while the driver contemplates the lack of passengers boarding at the St John's Road, Utley depot. Now the world of commercialisation had begun for unlike the electric trams the trackless carried advertisements, here for the 'Evening Post' and the Commercial Hotel and Cafe in Cavendish Street. The mechanism of this Garrett demonstration bus at Station Bridge appeared to be causing its operators some trouble on what could have been a trial run so it was a good thing that the road was empty at the time. The 'trackless', although limited by what would be termed today as unsightly overhead wires, did make a more flexible use of road space and it revolutionised passenger transport in the town. It allowed access to the town centre from the growing suburbs and consequently the demands of the town centre on terms providing better amenities for shopping, business, entertainment and leisure grew apace. The population of Keighley was increasing rapidly as the textile and engineering industries expanded. Families needed houses, schools, shops and reasonable access to them, hence this need for improved quality of the transport system. Keighley was not slow to respond and like most northern towns the corporation extended and improved its own service which was economical and comfortable. It instilled in its staff and passengers a sense of civic belonging and pride.

An array of holiday makers are about to set out from Cooke Lane at the start of Keighley 'Feast'. There is definitely an air of elegance about the young lady carrying her tennis racquet. No wonder the gentlemen on the kerb opposite are staring. Tickets have been booked, cases packed, raincoats are ready for use and the people of Keighley, or some of them, are ready to go.

All it needs are the white coated inspectors to ensure the West Yorkshire buses leave on time and then they are off. The tradition of Feast, or Wakes, in other northern industrial towns goes back further than this 1930s photograph. In Keighley at one time it was held at the end of July, then in September, before it moved to the horror of school administrators to the end of June.

The old idea of Feast was that factory masters before the advent of Bank Holidays would grant their workers a holiday at Christmas and at Whitsun and another at the time of local practice, which was Feast. That did not worry them too much for it was holidays without pay and it allowed for factory maintenance without any extra cost of paying workers for doing nothing.

The practice of going away for your holiday did not become really popular until the railways made it worthwhile to travel by train to the nearest seaside resort which was about the time of this photograph. So it is off to the sea or the country for these people who can afford to go away and it is stay at home for the many who can't, like possibly the spectators on the kerb.

A variety of wear as the staff of Keighley Corporation Tramways Department gather at the depot to 'celebrate' with a last photograph the end of the trackless car section in August 1932. It is noticeable here that there appears to be a sense of corporate identity as the pride in delivering an efficient transport system was a matter of honour in those days which ever position you held in the company from a 'suited' manager to a 'uniformed' conductor or driver to the 'overalled' mechanics although some drivers did regard themselves as 'kings'. This feeling for the company carried on for many years after this and working on the Keighley buses became a family affair. Employees included married couples, sons, daughters, brothers and sisters, almost like Keighley's version of 'Dynasty' without the nasty bits. The last trackless left with great ceremony at 11pm on 31st August 1932 with the Mayor, Alderman Michael Cryer at the wheel and the Chairman of the Transport Committee, Alderman Albert Smith, as the honorary conductor and to round off a memorable evening a large crowd gathered in the Municipal Hall for a final rendition of 'Auld Lang Syne'. Keighley had said farewell to its trams and its trolley buses in a matter of 30 years or so and embarked on a system of petrol and later diesel driven buses which has not really changed. The only changes have been in who or what provides the service and the ensuing debate concerns whether that service meets the needs of the community.

The first Guard House Estate trip was paid for by County Alderman JJ Brigg

Below: A chilly looking May day in the 1930s as mams and dads and grans and little brothers and sisters, too young to go, wave good bye to the children of Guard House Estate as they are soon to be off on their annual bus outing. Their first trip, organised by the estate's Social and Welfare Committee and paid for by County Alderman J J Brigg on whose land the estate was built after he had sold it to the corporation, was to Malham. The children and the volunteer supervisors had travelled in five coaches and walked, all two hundred of them, to the cove and then had their tea in Airedale Private Hotel. The Guard House Estate became mainly the home for, as officialdom termed it then, 'displaced persons'. Displaced only that the Corporation had decided to rid itself of totally inadequate town centre housing or slums, especially in the Westgate area and built estates at Broomhill, Highfield, Woodhouse and this one at Guard House where residents could enjoy 'the maximum hours of sunshine'. The first one hundred and twenty-eight houses were built in 1928 and soon the estate had its own schools, shops and churches and with the formation of the Social Committee trips like this and other events for adults and children alike were a regular feature of life there.

Above: The people in the queue waiting for the bus to Thwaites Brow could reflect that previously there would have been no shelter at all. The old station on Townfield Gate, cause of so much dissatisfaction, was demolished in 1939 with some property on the other side of the street leaving a square plot of land bounded by Adelaide Street, Bow Street and Queen Street for the new station.

In September 1940 the new station opened with buses running on sixteen routes but by 1961 it was obvious the new station was too small and conditions were chaotic with queues for one service getting mixed with queues for another, sometimes stretching on to the road. The answer was obvious. Build a new bus station. So came about the further new bus station.

The office block in the existing one was modernised. The rest of the work would be completed in three phases presumably to tie in with the town centre re-development. Long distance services were able to start from outside the booking office. Property on adjoining land was demolished and sensitive planning meant that the old station was successfully incorporated into the new one and it finally came into full use in November 1970.

The twenty-two terminus platforms meant that bus stops need no more cause a nuisance by being sited in nearby streets. It was conveniently adjacent to the multi storey car park and the central shopping area. There was now no need to go to Dewsbury to see a bus station as was suggested in 1939. After a long struggle Keighley's bus users now had their own.

All change!

Both pages: The advertisements in the local press in July 1968 contained the announcement that Yorkshire Bank branch in Keighley would open in its new premises in a modern and well equipped building on North Street on Monday July 22nd. The new development of Saturday opening, which had been adopted by all the major banks, would have another dimension - Friday evening opening between the hours of 5 and 7. The manager of the new premises was to be Mr N M Drury who would be very pleased to welcome old and new customers alike and so sandwiched between Barclays and Nat West with Elizabeth's ground floor shop for company, until it became the offices of a local estate agents, the bank opened for business. Its previous position had been across the road, nearly opposite, on the site of the original Mechanics Institute. The Institute had hired the building and neither the shape nor the structure has seriously altered in the intervening years. This was the scene from 1825 of lectures for the original members, of the provision of a library and opportunity to use scientific apparatus. You can imagine the excitement of those days at the chance to learn technical and scientific skills, as knowledge of the world around was available to men who had never had this experience before. That building would be at bursting point and it is no wonder that he original founders sought to purchase

their own premises where the space for learning, for experiment and for the acquisition of new skills could be carried out more conveniently and more comfortably. So in 1833 the Mechanics Institute moved along North Street to its newly built premises and the aims of those original pioneers took one more step forward.

The history of that building or of the Mechanics Institute would mean nothing to these two small boys one month after the bank left the old premises as they chased each other in the sunshine. Why

should it? They are on Summer Holiday and History lessons are for September, not August. If they did happen to look up they will have seen the Yorkshire Bank sign gone and an even closer look would make out the old sign of Yorkshire Penny Bank behind where the new one had been. But games are for playing! And what does it matter that the uphol- sterers has had to move out as well to the new Brunswick Arcade?

Now there's a place to chase each other; no cars there and no roads to cross. If those boys should have happened to have returned to North Street two

years later they would have seen a different sight. The shell of that old bank is still there. Lloyds Bank is still its neighbour. They would have been able to make out the Penny Bank sign above the centre front door and say that it continued to have an imposing entrance even though there is now fenced round as the demolition men remove its fine stonework and make the corner of Bow Street and North Street more attractive with flower beds and shrubs. And by then, two years older, they might have learned and appreciated that this corner was an important part of Keighley's past.

Both pictures: The end of an era as the Devonshire Street Congregational Chapel, opened in 1856 and regarded as one of the 'smarter' places in Keighley to worship, meets its end exactly one hundred and eight years later. The mill owners of Keighley would worship here and it would be quite a sight to see them and their ladies and children descending those stone steps to their awaiting carriages, the coachmen having sneaked out during the last hymn to prepare for their masters' arrival. A different sight it would be on other days in the week for Devonshire Street was also the venue for the Keighley cattle fair so the 'smart' place to be seen on Sunday would be populated by farmers and cows and all the other things associated with them on a weekday. The middle of the nineteenth century had witnessed a religious revival in this country with the biggest rise in church membership being experienced by the Baptists and the Independents, or as they were better known, the Congregationalists. By the time the Devonshire Street Chapel was built, there were nationally over 165,000 members. Interestingly the strength of membership was in the southern half of the country, especially in East Anglia and the central south. There was a subsequent steady rise in the north with a number of chapels like this one being built to accommodate the increase. After the Second World War there was an attempt to heal the long-standing division between the Presbyterians and the Congregationalists and that unity was achieved in 1972 as the United Reformed Church but by then this chapel had been erased from the map of Keighley and worshippers joined with those at the Christ Church in Spencer Street.

Another symbol of Keighley's past stands miserably waiting for the final push with an act of defiance from the ornate tower rather like a captain being last to leave his ship. The offices of the North Eastern Gas Board and once those of the municipal gas authority standing here on Cooke Lane since 1902 are ready to meet their fate as the move to re-model Keighley's town centre enters another phase. The Christmas rush of 1966 is not so evident here as the offices and showrooms and their neighbour, Direct Discount Stores, are closed. At least Direct went out in a flurry with its closing down sale attracting hundreds of people for the last of its many bargains. Queues stretched past the gas showrooms and round the corner into College Street as one of the trend-

setters of future retailing practices made its final contri-bution to shopping in this street. Standing in Cooke Lane today, or what is left of the original part, it is hard to imagine that buildings as dignified as the gas premises once stood here but in the move to bring a new image functional replaced dignity which is a pity. Keighley possessed some fine buildings. Many are still standing and are worth preserving as a reminder its past. It is said that history is the reservoir of human experience and planners and developers seem to forget that sometimes. The ancient Chinese had a curse which stated' May you live in interesting times', The 1960s were interesting times for the town but hopefully were not the forerunners of doom.

Left: The building that was Dickinson's, the drapers, has gone and the only consolation is that standing in front of Burgess's Garage now affords a better view of Cavendish Street. This empty space will soon house the multi-storey car park outlined in the town centre plan, close to the Airedale Shopping Centre and the bus station and on a different level to pedestrian traffic. The siting of shops at ground level under its parking floors did enable one important local shop to continue to function in the town centre. Reid's bookshop had been in the town since 1899 and the move to this premises took place in 1995. The garage of Walter Burgess has had an almost equally long connection with the town, being on Hanover Street since 1918. Apart from selling cars like Fords, the garage can boast that it supplied Fred of Fred's Ices fame with his unique ice-cream van with its giant cornet having the quality of a lighthouse beacon. Whether the garage wishes to take credit for that is another matter. It was at this time in the 1967 that the proposal to replace the Town Hall with a civic centre got past the talking stage into the planning stage. An exhibition showing a three-dimensional model with photographs and drawings was held in the lecture room of the library. The four storey building, to be sited on the North Street, Cavendish Street, Bow Street complex, was to be a 'centre for the community'. All seems to have come to naught, however, and Keighley retained its old Town Hall, probably adequate enough now that decisions are made in Bradford.

Below: The lady avoiding the rubble and debris and the improvised use of a discarded chair in Cooke Lane on this September day in 1961 appears none too concerned at the demise of Aaron King's Brewery but at the noise and the dust as another of Keighley's old buildings makes space for the new Airedale Centre. If a shopper stands in the vicinity of Argos, he or she will not be far off the King's old site.

King's was one of the town's breweries not to last the course, either because the 'big boys had brought them out or they closed out of economic necessity. King's pubs in the town included the Eastwood Tavern, Beaumonts and the Globe with the Low Street premises of the Golden Lion sold at public auction as far back as 1935.

Other local breweries included Cattle's at the Eastwood site in Dalton Lane which ceased trading in 1903, the even older Thompson's White Horse Brewery at New Road Side and the brewery operated by Jonathan Knowles at the recently closed Denholme Gate Inn. The flag is still being flown for the town by Timothy Taylor's which, despite the vast changes in the whole system of brewery ownership, keeps its independence while larger companies dominate the trade. It is heartening that many small breweries have survived and produced 'old fashioned' ale. As a result of their success and the pressure from groups such as Camra, the big firms have been forced to re-introduce ales made in this way but they have had to buy up many small concerns to do it.

A last glimpse of the remains of the Clock Tower above the old Mechanics Institute on North Street before it meets its fate. After the 1962 fire the shell of the old Mechanics Institute remained as a ruin for five more years. The Clock Tower was partially restored and still housed the famous clock. It had stood above the Institute since the turn of the century, erected in tribute to Prince Smith, father of Swire Smith, one of the champions of the adult education movement in the town.

As an industrial Keighley grew, it became the founders' aim to provide education and training to all adults irrespective of their background and circumstances in order that they should benefit from learning and the increase in new technical skills.

These Institutes were the forerunners of a massive expansion in educational facilities which resulted in the establishment of libraries, colleges and universities after the 1870 Education Act which had provided greater access to learning at the elementary school level.

This tower was an appropriate reminder of the work of those pioneers and stood as a focal point in the town for over 60 years until the it was decided to demolish it. It was said that when masonry and the surrounding scaffolding fell into North Street, causing only damage to an electric lamp standard, fortunately, it was the tower's protest at such an undignified exit after such a dignified life.

Below: Construction work was well under way in Cooke Lane when this picture was taken. It is believed to date from the late 1960s. A sturdy dumper truck and concrete mixer are evidence to the work in progress on the normally busy street. Local people had to endure considerable inconvenience for a number of years while the architects and builders re-shaped Keighley's shopping facilities. We can only guess at what the little lad on the right of the picture was saying to his mum. He is smartly wrapped up against the cold, complete with balaclava which rekindles memories of the warm but often itchy feeling they caused to us as youngsters. Still, in the days before almost everyone seemed to own a car, we were all glad of any means to keep the cold out during our long waits at the bus stop. During the work along Cooke Lane the old *North Eastern Gas* offices and popular *Direct Walk Round Store* were pulled down. Much of the redevelopment in this part of Keighley was undertaken by the Murrayfield organisation.

Right: The traditional unique frontage that was Montagu Burtons, Tailor of Taste, looks forlornly down Market Street from its Low Street site. Burton' architectural style was easily recognisable wherever a man, and his wife, shopped for his clothes. The black stone often found at the sides of the shop and underneath the main display window was imported from Norway and was called affectionately, but not geologically accurately, as 'Burtonite'. The grandness of its upper floors in many of its branches contained a ballroom or a billiard and later snooker hall, or sometimes both, and was the scene of many a mis-spent youth, it is reputedly said.

Burton's will give way to the re-launching of Queen Street as Queensway and the entrance to the Airedale Centre. Next to Burton's is Marks and Spencer which first came to Keighley in 1912. The shop we can just see in this photograph was extensively modernised in 1935 and in the new look Keighley there would still be a shop, the presence of which is valued by every town. If there is a Marks and Spencer it is worth visiting to shop or worth investing in as a prospective shop owner. The closer your shop is to Marks, the more likely you are to succeed is one popular theory. A pity Burton's did not think that way.

Shopping spree

The stylish glass canopy which stretched lower down the street was certainly its trademark

The cinema posters are blank in this 1960 photograph of the North side of Cavendish Street but at that time the street itself was prospering. L.A.Holmes, with branches throughout the region. selling knitting wool and ladies' fashions, was typical of the many shops who were a vital part of the street's business life then. The stylish glass canopy which stretched lower down this side of the street was certainly its trademark and gave it an elegance which was to rival the Burlington Arcade of nearby North Street. The street had an air of grace and dignity befitting its lordly name and was, and probably still is, at least on this north side, a place to see and be seen. The movement away from small independent traders or businesses with one establishment or like Holmes with branches locally had not at this time caught on and shops like O.S.Wain, Maison Maude, Barretts Chemist, Baldwins, Foulds Garage could remain in the area for some years yet.

What ever happened to the York Medical and Surgical Company advertising Everest and Jennings Folding Wheelchairs is not certain. Both shops, like Dickinson's opposite, eventually did not survive the march of progress in this part of the street and were demolished.

The junction of Low Street and Brunswick Street is still in September 1962 dominated by the Keighley Co-operative Society buildings. The Yorkshire Evening News announces that the Labour party is in trouble although it cannot have been as dire as the one facing the Conservative government of Harold McMillan in that July when in the 'night of the long knives' seven cabinet ministers were sacked. Parking is no problem for the Morris 1000 car, then termed a 'shopping basket on wheels', today a collector's item and surely one of the most reliable and popular of cars being built by what was then a thriving British car industry. A society like the Co-op which aimed to satisfy all its member's needs was a dominant force in Keighley's shopping world and could boast that it could supply anything and everything and like supermarkets today had its own brand named goods. Before the war it had built its own abattoir in Parkwood Street and the butchery department demonstrated 'the true co-op principle of providing a thoroughly good article apart from the mere consideration of the profit derivable from it'. The manager regularly attended cattle markets at Leeds, Skipton and Long Preston and even visited Craven farms to chose suitable beasts. But 1962 was the time of the rise of self-service stores and it is to Keighley Co-op's credit that it could compete with them and prosper in its new stores in the town centre.

Above: It is 3.35pm on a October day in 1962 and the corner of Coney Lane and Low Street and East Parade is an empty part of Keighley. The road over Low Bridge to Harden and Cullingworth does not have the same feeling of restriction and movement it has today. Worth Way has transformed the area as much as the new buildings which have replaced Edna Sexton's hair stylists, the Milliners, the Stocking Shop, the Wool Shop and the Jewellers next to it. The movement to change was gathering pace at this time and the effect it had on the businesses like clothing shops was profound for people's tastes in clothing had rapidly altered. Clothes were now mass-produced with the result that 'popular fashions' were sold at popular prices for both men and women. Shops like Burtons were a typical example as they changed their image, their frontages and became one of many selling to an increasingly demanding public. Ladies' fashions underwent the bigger change. The then 'immoral' mini skirt had a lasting effect as hemlines became shorter even for the more mature lady and shops were either left with unsaleable stocks or they moved

with the times. The Stocking Shop will now be selling tights, which have superseded stockings. They had to otherwise the mini-skirt would have been too revealing. 'Fashion', which had 'arrived' for young people in the late 50s and early 60s created not one style but styles. This created a dilemma for the young ladies of the time concerning not only what was 'in' but having to try to persuade parents not to be so old-fashioned and understand the need to 'with it'.

Top: The north side of High Street between Chapel Lane and West Lane on a wet day at the beginning of January 1968 shows that over the many years that it has functioned as a bus and car route there has not been much change to its lay out. The recent changes that have taken place are the clearing of the property in Turkey Street. The changes which did seriously affect this part of Keighley occurred much earlier than this when High Street, one of the oldest streets in the town, was not as open as it is in this photograph. The nearby Westgate area of the town had been one of the most densely populated districts with housing totally inadequate to meet the basic needs of their dwellers and caused the Health Authorities no end of concern. In the 1930s there was a massive programme of slum clearance in which every thing went including houses the, abattoir and South Street Corn Mills. Also to go was the Friends' Meeting House although by then the Quakers had already moved to Skipton Road. To rehouse the people who had to leave the council built estates like the one up West Lane at Guard house. This area over this period of time in the 1930s took on a different complex and one which has remained. High Street has become a more pleasant place to work and to shop in. Traffic has been able to move more freely and the subsequent building of a car park has made pedestrian and motor access easier.

Below: In the interim period between the old market being closed, waiting to be pulled down, and the new covered market and car park being built the town had a temporary one. Many of the traders of the original market were encouraged enough to keep up the tradition of selling and for a limited period.

It was not expected that the atmosphere of the old would remain. The noise of the stallholders as they voiced their bargains and bantered with each other would be muted. There would be no basket stacking contests as occurred between the wars or barrel rolling races.

This market was functional before the much heralded new arrived. Whether the replacement was looked forward to by those who worked and shopped in the old is debatable but in June 1971 the modern covered Keighley market opened it did, the ceremony being performed by the Mayor, Alderman Sydney Bancroft.

It had been built at a cost of £134,000 with, it was claimed, 'state of the art facilities'. At its entrance was the Fire and Wheel symbol which was to represent the energy and mechanical power of Keighley's historical industry built from a prize winning design by teenage student, Angela Pettit. The old tradition was being carried on. There was record trading for the first few months and Keighley proved it truly was a market town.

Left: The 1960s brought about a revolution in consumer spending and with it came a multiplication of the number of shops willing to accommodate this phenomenon. While many small family businesses struggled, there came the rise of the self-service grocery store and old market leaders like the Home and Colonial Group and even the Co-op fell behind the rapidly expanding Sainsbury chain and John Cohen's Tesco. Relative newcomers like Asda and Morrisons emerged and towns gave them active encouragement to build new stores often away from the headache of the town centre. Here we see construction underway on the recently developed Worth Way of the first Morrison's store to be built outside of Bradford and at the time Keighley's largest retail store. Using recently developed building materials and methods, the store, pictured here in July 1968, was opened for business in the following October. Shoppers were promised quick service, maybe not as personal as they were used to, with 18 modern check-outs, over 120 staff, wide aisles for wide shopping trolleys, a coffee bar and ample parking. The floor space for the technically minded customer was to be 58,000 square feet and the total cost of building came to £275,000. Thus began a change in the shopping habits of the people of Keighley and with the advent of other stores there has been no let up in the demand for the shopper's custom.

Above: The Famous Army Stores unique sale viewed from the top of the market with the Parish Church in the background and an almost empty street. Like many other northern industrial towns in the late 1950s and early 1960s Keighley was beginning to experience a change in the pattern of industry, maybe not as severe as some of its neighbours but there were established town centre firms which were declining or moving elsewhere. New businesses mostly found cheap sites outside the centre and by doing this they avoided the problem of difficulty of access and transport and also found it easier to gain planning permission. Soon parts of town centres showed signs of wear and tear and even some of decay. It may not have been evident at the time to people in this area like the shop owners and the people who lived and worked here but in retrospect the decision to redevelop especially before the sense of hopelessness, which affected other towns and cities set in, was indeed a sensible one. Small family businesses, like Stanley's and Shackleton's possibly, however well regarded, were struggling in face of stiff competition. The town's landscape needed a breath of life. Whatever was planned had to accommodate an increase in people's spending power and a transformation in what they ate, how they dressed and spent their leisure. The need for changes to what amenities the town could offer was clear; what was not clear what was the changes should look like.

For over 600 years Keighley Market has been an important part of the town's economy

The last gasp of the traditional market area of Keighley in 1970. On this site since 1833 and having had a charter for over 600 years Keighley market had for long time been an important part of the town's economy where shoppers could look for bargains stalls like Jerry's before they move on to Gerry's stall for more bargains and there is an air of busy-ness about the place.

The hotch potch arrangement of the goods on display is unimportant compared to the bargains undoubtedly on offer. The market has been for generations of shoppers and traders a focal part of the community and more than just a shopping site. It has its own unique atmosphere that was social as well as commercial almost like a club. Its closeness to the town centre and its accessibility to public transport gave it a permanence that the town appreciated throughout the year. On this cold February day the selection of footwear by these shoppers range from keeping out the cold and wet utility style to keeping out the cold and wet fashion style.

Above: Television in the 1960s, the newest form of entertainment, carried all before it. Electrical shops like Curry's boomed and like the hire-purchase industry which was expanding rapidly so was the number of television rental companies. On to Low Street came shops like D.E.R. and Rentaset and others who were often branches of television manufacturers who had found another profitable outlet for their products. Independent Television, which in 1955 had broken the BBC's monopoly and was funded by advertising, grew and grew and by 1962 was available in nearly every home in the country and those H-shaped television aerials, as we can see here on the roof above the Famous Army Stores, were part of the national landscape. Think back to the advertisements on television in the 1960s for soap powder and cornflakes. Remember the ones for cigarettes when we were persuaded by a sincere sounding actor or actress that smoking was *the* way to appear sophisticated or THE way to attract a member of the opposite sex. Recall the cartoon and jingle type ones such as 'Keep going well, keep going Shell, You can be sure of Shell, Shell, Shell.' Advertising certainly quickened the pace of the consumer revolution. Local shops like Newbys specialists in game and poultry and fresh fruit which once relied on their good name to sell their goods now began to face competition from nationally owned shops and stores selling nationally owned products.

Right: One of the great survivors or winners in the national economic battlefield has been Boots the Chemist. Like Thomas Lipton who started with one shop and £100 and then had 500 within 45 years, Jesse Boot with his 'pure drugs' followed the same technique of bulk buying, cheap selling, a large turnover and mass advertising.

Soon there was a Boots in almost every town. The range of goods and services on offer these days makes Boots an essential part of any town's commercial life and presumably where Boots goes others will follow. It is interesting that there is another branch of the Co-op here and like Stylo a branch remained on the same site for some years after this 1962 photograph.

It was about this time that the Co-operative movement faltered, caught between its commitment to small community or specialist shops and the competition with the ever increasing large chain stores. It has remained a force to be reckoned with, however, and the evidence is there in Keighley.

The same can be said about Boots - look at the importance and the size of its branch in the Airedale Centre. It has always managed to retain a prominent position in the town; in this photograph it is at the junction with Cooke Lane when that street was one of the premier shopping streets in Keighley.

It is always interesting to look at a view of a part of any town which has been vastly changed or just disappeared and have a mental quiz as to where the shops and businesses were exactly and what did ever happen to them. Two views of Lawkholme Crescent taken on the same day in October 1962 shows this part of Keighley between Cavendish Street and Queen Street as a small but vital part of the town's business life. The number of pedestrian shoppers, however, can be almost counted as 'one man and his dog' as they pass Wild's bakers and confectioners which fortunately still survives. In fact it has prospered disproving a theory that family businesses cannot compete against the 'big boys'. Ryley's stationers with its circulating library dominated the Cavendish Street corner but like its branch in Halifax it is not part of the town's scene. Lakeland Cleaners has added Pennine to its name but there is no branch in Keighley. Pearson's was the butchers. Bridgefield was a busy textile shop and Brown and Berry newsagents and tobacconist. But what about Smith Bros? And Zip? Can you remember going to the dentist above Ryley's? Or the barbers, with his traditional pole, above Wild's? The delivery van has a very interesting message' Reward through Service'. One poignant part of this view is what has gone already for at the junction with Queen Street are the walls of the Queen's Theatre or what's left of them.

Left: The Christmas decorations in January 1971 are still up in Wilson's Nurseryland in High Street which catered for the needs of Keighley's very young for two generations or so here and round the corner in Chapel Street. Compared to the rest of the town very little has changed in High Street to the buildings themselves - 'only the names have been changed'. Wilson's is on the site where Driver's Millinery Shop stood in the 1920s. Smith's is where Tillotsons used to trade although its roof does need to quickly seen to judging by this photograph. The double fronted Smith's shop served mainly tobacco products until at least 1975 and possibly beyond that. There would be today very few shops which would or could remain such a specialised business for reasons such as the apparent move away from smoking as a desirable social activity and the advent of multi-product, low-cost stores. It is a matter of great interest that the shops and businesses on High Street so close to the new development in Keighley centre should continue to prosper and the tradition of a shop specialising in selling babywear items and prams continues today although with a different proprietor, despite the increase in competition and the temptation to do your shopping under one roof.

Above: Lawkholme Crescent in 1967 before the changes with the bus station and Ramsbottoms electrical shop in the background. Pearsons, the butchers, is showing signs of wear and tear although you can still buy your shoes at Brogans and your Senior Service tipped and Daily Mail at Berry's with a choice of 'Woman' or 'Woman's Realm' if you so wish. What is very interesting here is the Wonderloaf, not the van but the name of the bread for it states that even though this product is far superior to other makes, there is no increase in price for that extra quality. There had always been a tradition in this country of small private bakers until the 1950s when firms like Spillers introduced 'Wonderloaf' and Rank and then Westons came with their own brands, 'Mother's Pride' and 'Sunblest'. Prices were kept down and quality was standardised. This move to mass production put many small bakers out of business or being taken over by larger companies.

If it was possible to count the number of small bakers in the Keighley area before the 1950s and after then, it might make an interesting comparison. Many did survive, however, and continue to do so today satisfying an increasing demand for, amongst other things, crusty bread, baked in the traditional way.

At work

Above: Built originally on land purchased in 1825 from Lord George Cavendish at Low Bridge the Keighley Local Board of Health was prevented from any further expansion of its gasworks when the Great Northern Railway proposed building a line from Keighley to Halifax and bought the surrounding land. The new gas works were then consequently erected at Thwaites in 1876 and the occasion was deemed worthy of a celebration with a six course dinner at the Devonshire Hotel. On the menu were such delicacies as calf's head, roast hare and grouse. The old Low Bridge retort house was later transformed into the town's fire station and much to the disgust of the Great Northern Railway the railway line to Halifax had to be re-sited when it was discovered that the trains were too long for the platforms! Here in 1914 further improvements are being made to Keighley's gas supply with gas holder number three being built and we see the holder in the course of construction. The second photograph is a picture of it complete in all its glory with two volunteers half way up acting as a reference for its immense size. The holders had a capacity of 750,000 cubic feet and when in 1930 one of them caught fire, the top blew off and that volume of gas escaped in little over a minute. In the early years of Keighley providing its own gas charges were based upon the number of jets in the house or the business. The charge was £1 per jet, per year. The gas supply was cut off each night at 10 o'clock while from mid-May until mid-September there was none available at all.

Right: It is a good thing there were in 1924 few Health and Safety regulations for the method of securing the scaffolding or ensuring the workmen's safety would be called into question as the last bits of the town's War Memorial are placed in position. The memorial had replaced the railed circle of trees in the middle of the Town Hall Square. The stone for it was locally quarried at Eastburn and the bronze figures were the work of sculptor, Henry Fehr of South Kensington in London. On the side of the memorial facing the Town Hall were placed in bronze the former coats of arms of Keighley, composed of the combined crests of the De Kighley and Cavendish families, lords of the manor for several generations. The symbol of victory and peace is the laurel wreath while the soldier and sailor on the plinth reflect the horrors of the 'war to end all wars', the 1914 to 1918 war which claimed the lives of a generation including 900 young men of Keighley. The erection of this memorial was partly a reminder that such an sacrifice should never be made again and another reminder of what was lost. Over £6,000 was raised by public subscription to pay for the statue and in front of 25,000 people the Keighley War Memorial was unveiled in December 1924 in an appropriate position in the centre of the town.

A team photograph for the shift of the bayonet room at the Burlington Shed of Prince-Smith and Stells Ltd of Dalton Lane during World War II. Britain's mobilisation of women for the Battle for Production went further than every country apart from Russia. This was a natural consequence of the men being called to the fighting front. A popular song of the time sums it up: 'She's the girl that makes the thing, That drills the holes that holds the spring, That drives the rod that turns the knob, That works the thingamabob.......And it's the girl that makes the thing, That holds the oil that oils the ring, That works the thingamabob THAT'S GOING TO WIN THE WAR'

Women went to work in aircraft factories, engineering sheds, chemical plants, munitions

factories like the 'Dump' at Stetson and filled the traditional male jobs on public transport, delivering the post, working on the railway, collecting rent and delivering milk and bread. They joined the Women's Land Army where they were paid £1.85 for a fifty hour working week (much more hours at harvest time) but eighty thousand did volunteer. It was the three hundred and sixty-five Keighley WVS members who freely volunteered to work with the ARP, who helped with evacuees, served in hospitals and works' canteens and looked after hospital supplies. And it was those ladies, with the help of a man or two, who boosted Prince-Smith and Steel's workforce from one thousand seven hundred to three thousand five hundred and made among other things 1,057,515 spike bayonets!

Above: The threat of German invasion of this island at the beginning of the second World War in 1940 was real and led to the formation of the Local Defence Volunteers later renamed the Home Guard. Keighley boasted its own Dad's Army and many local firms had their own contingent. The beauty of the television series was it was based on the situation as it existed at that perilous time, albeit it was extremely wittily written and produced. Here we see the staff of the Keighley - West Yorkshire Bus Services outside their Anvil Street premises undergoing arms drill. Fortunately their new found skills were never put to the real test but it was all serious stuff. In August 1941 Keighley was the scene of mock battle. The Home Guard was deployed to defend the town's key points from attack by members of the Regular Army whose soldiers posed as saboteurs and as enemy parachutists in a variety of disguises. One report stated there was 'fierce fighting in the town'. The locals seemed to have acquitted themselves well and proved more than adequate at interrogations and traffic control. As the threat of invasion receded, the four Keighley Home Guard detachments were 'stood down' and their final parade took place in December 1944 at a march past along North Street.

Right: So this is where it all could have happened - the Borough Engineer's office in College Street. This must be

the place where the planning to re-develop the town took place. Then it would a bigger hive of industry than it appears here. By now, 1966, Keighley is in the middle of the work to carry out these plans, and the engineer will combine the need to preserve the commercial life of the town with the need to oversee the implementation of the process. At this time Keighley had a greater political autonomy than it does today and even at this time there was the talk of the re-organisation of local government. The Redcliffe-Maude Commission, set up by the Labour government, in the same year was already paving the way for the political map of Britain to be re-drawn, with changes to make the administration of local government more efficient. The commission will recommend that there should be two sorts of authority - county councils and district councils. Added to them will be six metropolitan councils in the highly populated industrial areas, including West Yorkshire, and within them would be metropolitan boroughs. Bradford will be one and Keighley part of it, so it will lose whatever independence it possessed when the re-organisation takes place in 1972 and 1973. The irony of it all is as we return to the Keighley Borough Engineer's office is that in the re-development of the town that office had to go. And the office that oversaw the rebuilding of Keighley with structures to last for years took one lunchtime for the demolition workers to pull down.

A precision line-up of office staff in the NSF works in 1947. And a very interesting calendar on the wall. And he is the only one in this office, it would seem, to have the authority of a telephone. The firm, British National Switch Factory, had arrived in Keighley in 1940 after being bombed out of its premises in Croydon. The 'Switch People' acquired this Ingrow Bridge site in 1946, employing then about eight hundred people. Interestingly at the same time another of the town's eventual major employers also set up in business as another firm had come north to escape London's bombing. Bagcraft, whose speciality was army webbing, stayed here until the end of the war then it moved to Dundee. Its manager remained in Keighley and Peter Black took over a small Keighley-based manufacturer of bags and webbing products and very soon it had established an enviable reputation beyond local boundaries for high quality leather goods. Despite the traumas of rationing and fuel shortages, Britain's industries, traditional or recently established, made surprising progress in those post-war years as everywhere there was a demand for manufactured goods which had been unavailable or in short supply in war time. The result was a boom which allowed firms like NSF and Blacks to prosper. It is hard to imagine now when selling and marketing are essential departments in an organisation or firm that in those years selling was hardly necessary. Then customers were queuing for goods. For a long time cars fetched higher prices second hand than new, as manufacturers could not make enough to satisfy the demand. So the office workers at NSF have a bright future in front of them as they work hard in what was then a bright modern office.

Left: The bus station is on the left and at the corner of Cooke Lane and Bow Street stands Weatherheads solicitors and in 1960 these offices appear to be a permanent feature of the landscape of Keighley town centre. Within five years Weatherheads had moved to Devonshire Street to make way for the new Airedale Centre and the street which once housed Timothy Taylor's brewery and later some of the famous names in Keighley business and commercial history either closed or were re-sited as Changegate, Cooke Lane and Towngate were replaced by the centre.

This re-development was carried out in stages so that the old shops and businesses could move as each new area was completed. The plans for this development had been rigorous with borough councillors and officers having visited Shipley, Wakefield and Crewe to obtain information on town centre development. As far back as 1962 the Murrayfield Real Estate Company Limited were chosen to carry it out in Keighley. The company assured people of 'their positive approach to planning and reconstruction' and would be 'opening vistas to buildings worthy of retention with an attractive pedestrian shopping precinct free from the hazards of vehicular traffic' A hundred shops were planned with the whole venture not scheduled to be completed until 1969.

So Keighley began to make a response to the demands made by increasing traffic, the move to the suburbs for housing and the need for greater accessibility to the town's amenities.

Below: Imagine the conversation between these three young men as they survey what is left of the clinic on Westgate. It will be nothing to do with the better view they now have of Springfield Mills on Becks Road or of North Beck Mills right behind the old clinic. Nor would they want to discuss the new multi-storey car park to be erected here or how North Beck was covered over in the 1930s. The history of the clinic might have interested them for they would no doubt have been a visitor to that 'art decor' building for jabs or their orange juice sometime in their brief lives.

They would learn that Health Care in the 1960s was very different to when the clinic was built. Today they would not have to pay for treatment or their parents join a contributory scheme to ensure that hospital treatment was there in an emergency for the family. They would learn that the National Health Service ensured that there was free treatment for all. That they could have the pleasure of the school dental service and the school nurse trying to pull your hair out as she searches for nits. That they could go to the doctors when they had a sore throat and the cost of that awful medicine was nil. That all this was possible not out of charity but out of the state's concern for the nation's welfare.

These lads would learn all this and more and then as they survey what is left of their clinic they might when play quite happily among the rubble for that is the only reason why they are there surely.

Below: It is April 1967 and work to bring to earth the remains of the Municipal Hall, once the Keighley Mechanics Institute, is well under way. The Hall had at one time housed the Art School of Keighley Technical College and was home to

the town, remained as a reminder of a famous landmark in Keighley's heritage until March 1967, one month before this photograph was taken.

Left: This charming mill formed an important part of the lives of many

part of Keighley Boys' Grammar School. The original institute had been on this site since 1833 as it sought to provide access to knowledge and learning to all and not just the privileged few. At the turn of the century the Institute became known as the Technical College as the need to expand its educational activities grew apace. The hall took on a new lease of life. It acquired another role in the town and became the venue for important civic occasions. It became a major centre for many a social function, for meetings, for firms to entertain their staff. It became a popular dance hall from rock and roll to ballroom until the fateful early morning of Sunday 3rd March 1962. After a dance the previous evening the building went up in flames, the result, it was believed, of a discarded cigarette. The shell of the Mechanics Institute, pioneer of adult education in

thousands of local workers over many years. Of course, they didn't all work there at the same time, and in the year this picture was taken the quaint property was the home of Denby Brothers Ltd, the well-known Keighley textile spinners. *Denby's* were noted for the quality of their crossbred and merino products according to the advertising sign fixed on the wall of the mill. Keighley was world famous for textile products. Originally cotton processing was the main pursuit of the scores of local mills but later this was overtaken in economic importance by worsted production. In 1880 Keighley accounted for about 10% of England's growing worsted production. This photograph was taken in the mid 1960s, it being possible to 'date' the picture by looking at the selection of motor vehicles parked on either side of the scene.

MKU 7 would be a money earner in today's fad of having personalised number plates on your car or your 4x4. The only thing that was personalised in this 1962 photograph of Hanover Street are the Keighley Co-operative Society buildings. Established in the early nineteenth century to ensure that every member did receive a 'personalised service' the Co-operative movement had spread from its humble origins in Toad Lane in Rochdale to the extent that by 1914 it had three million members and a turnover even then of £88 million. In prospering northern working class communities the Co-op was the main if not the only store and the Keighley Co-op could, and did, provide every kind of service for its members - the dairy, the abattoir, the bakery, the undertaking service, the chemist, insurance, the cafe, the bank, the travel agent, the coal merchant - a contemporary welfare state. The Keighley Co-op could set up branches in outlying parts of the town and further afield and was the dominant force until the middle of this century. It will not be long before this dairy will be pulled down but a new Co-op will open in 1966 proving the mutual faith between the town and the modern Co-operative movement still exists.

A few onlookers could gaze through the fence four months after work began on clearing the site of the fire five years previously at the Municipal Hall and on a massive expansion of the facilities Keighley Technical College could offer. By 1954 there had been a serious shortage of teaching accommodation and it was necessary to open an annexe in the old Temple Street schoolrooms. Another annexe was opened in Strawberry Street two years later and in 1968 the college's main building was opened at the junction of North Street and Cavendish Street, the plan for which was incorporated into the re-development programme for the whole of the town centre. This was a steel framed structure faced with Yorkshire stone containing enough glass to give adequate daylight to rooms. All this was a far cry from the days of the old Mechanics Institute but a natural development of the pioneering work of the original founders who had the foresight to realise that it was the right of every young person to receive a decent education and training. So that little girl on the corner has a lot to be thankful for as she gazes at the college and the site of the founding of Keighley education, although she would not have known it at the time and no doubt had more important things on her mind!

A mixture of old and new in this August 1967 photograph of the top of Cavendish Street before it meets North Street.

The extension to the Technical College is well under way stretching round to Lord Street as the re-development of this area takes shape. Behind the Lakeland Laundry van the Keighley Library can be made out. Now a listed building the library is a fine example of what can be done in the way of preserving all that is worthwhile in a town. It was built in 1904, the first in England to be funded by the American philanthropist, Andrew Carnegie. who gave £10,000 towards the cost and for his generosity the Freedom of the Borough was conferred on him and the spacious reading room was originally called the Andrew Carnegie Free Library.

The library was extended in 1961 to include then a Children's Library and Lecture Hall. Across the other side of Albert Street can be seen the dome, or cupola, and the weather vane with its squirrel of the old Temperance Hall, meeting place of many a Keighley group or society but now dedicated to Bingo.

A sign of the times in the advertising hoardings is that there is a shortage of nurses in 1967 as, nationally, questions are asked as to how to provide public services which the country has a right to expect, a debate the pioneers of the old Mechanics Institute might have wished to have contributed to.